FLIGHT OF THE QUETZAL MAMA

FLIGHT OF THE QUETZAL MAMA

HOW TO RAISE LATINO SUPERSTARS AND GET THEM INTO THE BEST COLLEGES

Roxanne Ocampo

ISBN: 1532960166
ISBN 13: 9781532960161

Other books by Roxanne Ocampo

Nailed it!
Quetzal Mama's Toolkit
for Extraordinary College Essays

El Vuelo de la Mamá Quetzal:
Cómo Criar Hijos Exitosos y
Prepararlos para las Mejores Universidades

Betcha Didn't Know!
Quetzal Mama's Tips
for *Latino* Parents

TABLE OF CONTENTS

Dedication

To the brave parents who've always had wings,
and now prepare to soar.

Acknowledgments

Arturo Ocampo, My Husband—Thank you for always supporting me *unconditionally* in my Quetzal Mama goals. If it wasn't for your support, I could not have completed the books, programs, or tools that have helped thousands. Thank you also for helping me raise three beautiful children and giving them your unconditional love and support.

Carlos, Gabi, and Emilio, My Children— I'm still amazed, every day, by your strength, determination, and hard work, and by your commitment to serve marginalized communities. I am so very proud of you all and blessed to have been given the opportunity to be your Quetzal Mama, your "Pfunky Bus" Chauffeur, and part of your amazing journey.

Ruben and Josie Gutierrez, My Parents—Thank you for instilling in me the curiosity to write and for encouraging me to use this gift to serve others.

Margarita Maestas-Flores, My Editor –Thank you for sharing your extraordinary talents and "wicked" editing skills! You took a manuscript and turned it into a *real* book.

Dr. Eileen Barrett, English Professor, California State University, East Bay—Thank you for encouraging me to pursue the discipline of English. I am now able to share my thoughts, in written form, with the world.

To all Quetzal Mamas throughout the U.S. and Latin America —
thank you for using and sharing the tips and strategies in this book with
your children and within your communities. Together we are raising
Superstars and ensuring more Latino students are successfully transitioning to colleges and universities.

ABOUT THE AUTHOR

QUETZAL MAMA IS the pen name and brand of Roxanne Ocampo. Roxanne is a proud *mamá Latina*, author, blogger, public speaker, and full time college admission consultant. She has published several popular books focused on helping Latino parents navigate the complicated college admissions process.

As Founder and CEO of Quetzal Mama™, she runs the non-profit Quetzal Mama Scholars™ – a college admission coaching program for students in eight North San Diego County school districts.

Since 2010, she has successfully coached thousands of students throughout the US. Having designed a unique, culturally relevant curriculum of more than 75 college workshop topics, and specialized College Boot Camps for K-5, middle school, high school, and community college students (and their parents), she teaches strategies for college admission and competitive scholarships. Every year the students from her practice earn admission to the most selective universities and are honored as national scholarship recipients.

She also provides consulting services for many organizations including private and public colleges and universities, K-12 public school districts, community based organizations, college-going organizations, Migrant Education, ELAC/DELAC, and student organizations.

She is a third year Doctoral Candidate at UC San Diego where she received a full Fellowship. She is currently conducting a Phenomenological Case Study concerning first generation, low-income, high-performing, Mexican-American students from Arizona, California, and Texas, who recently matriculated into a highly selective college. She holds a Master's Degree and Bachelor's Degree in English – where she learned her unique craft of writing. The theories and philosophy that guide her work are situated in Critical Race Theory.

Born and raised in the Bay Area (San Jose) Roxanne resides with her family in San Marcos, California. Roxanne is married to Dr. Arturo E. Ocampo—a Civil Rights and Education Law Attorney, and an expert in Diversity & Educational Equity for public and private universities and California community colleges. Together they have raised three incredible children following the 10 Quetzal Mama Principles.

Introduction

THERE IS NOTHING like watching your child's reaction when they click open the virtual "big envelope." That envelope contains six words they've worked their entire academic career to earn: *"Welcome to the Incoming Freshman Class!"*

In our world, the big envelope happens very infrequently. When one of our Latino students gains access to higher academia, our entire community embraces and salutes that student. This is unquestionably a unique reaction compared to other cultural groups. We feel proud and joyful, even though we may not know the student. For us, this student symbolizes hope.

Our reaction is unique because our Latino children are unique. Our children have unique perspectives and unique challenges. Their path to higher education (including the Ivy Leagues) is significantly different than their white or Asian counterparts. The academic strategy for our children is not shared by any other group. As such, when our students apply for admission to colleges, they are considered through a unique lens that respects their unique qualifications and life experiences. *Finally,* at the highest level of academia, our children will be valued for the unique set of life experiences they bring to a college campus.

Our children are also unique because Latino students do not fall into the same broad category as their counterparts with respect to admission policies and practices. There are programs, resources, and scholarships specifically earmarked for Latino students. Our students have unique advantages not publicized or documented. Unless we are aware of these resources, our child may miss the opportunity to take full advantage.

Be cautious when you read the above paragraphs. Your Latino child's unique path to college (including the Ivy Leagues) has nothing to do with benefitting from Affirmative Action, a lowered academic benchmark, or being a token anything. An incorrect assumption many persons make (including many highly educated persons) is that the academic benchmark is *lower* for Latino and other "minority" students. This is simply untrue. In fact, it is the opposite. The benchmark is often *higher* for underrepresented students because of the obstacles they are required to overcome—obstacles their white and Asian counterparts do not encounter.

Some of the obstacles our bright Latino students must overcome include:

- Growing up without resources or knowledge of a pathway to college and/or the Ivy Leagues;
- Being first in the family to go to college;
- Belonging to a lower socio-economic class;
- Speaking English as a second language (for themselves and/or their parents);
- Being perceived by others as inferior—a bias that impacts academic opportunities and outcomes;
- Lowering of self-image—the result of internalizing the pervasive stereotypes that manifest through the behaviors and attitudes of teachers, administrators, and society;
- Lacking culturally relevant role models, mentors, or counselors;
- Being tracked into programs inconsistent with their intellectual abilities; and
- Being overlooked, bypassed, or excluded from programs that *are* consistent with their intellectual abilities (for example the GATE Program), due to cultural bias and stereotypes.

Given the same standardized test scores, the same GPA, and the same teachers, a Latino student will often have a completely different academic experience and outcome compared to white and Asian counterparts.

When our Latino students do succeed, it is typically the result of a phenomena I call *Resilient Rodrigo*. Rodrigo will have to "prove" himself over and over, because along his academic journey he will face a new group of uninformed and biased people every step of the way. Rodrigo will inevitably encounter these obstacles each school year, with each application to a prestigious and competitive academic program, and with each new teacher. Ironically, the resilience built over years of encountering these cycles, and the requirement to always outperform his peers, will ultimately become an asset to Rodrigo. His resilience will place him in the top of his class and potentially earn recognition from Ivy League schools and competitive universities. This resilience factor is how many Latino children gain entrance into these prestigious institutions—not through lowered SAT scores or lowered GPAs.

Because of these challenges, and our unique pathway to the university, I decided to write this book. Now, this is not a "You Can Do It" book that seeks to convince or motivate you to get your child to college. I already know Latino parents are incredibly inspired and motivated to help their children succeed. I am convinced Latino parents are not looking to understand *why* their children should go to college but *how* to get them there. This book is not about the *why*, but the *how*.

As I began the process of strategizing my own children's road to college, I quickly learned two things. First, there is not a single, comprehensive book that provides Latino parents with a plan of action to help their children succeed academically from K-5, middle, and high school, through college. Second, unless parents have the "inside track" and know the right people, or are connected with the right resources, they will miss out on academic opportunities for their children.

This book is the outgrowth of everything I documented along my journey of navigating the maze of academia. This was partly due to my hyper-organized nature—but mostly because I wanted something in writing I could share with other parents. I spent more than ten years completing my independent research; talking with teachers, parents, counselors, principals, and superintendents; and reading books about college admissions. I started doing this when my children were in elementary school, and I never stopped. Since I could not find a book or resource specifically addressing Latino children and a plan of action to help them succeed academically, I decided to write one myself.

In addition to helping my own kids get through the college process, the writing of this book was also influenced by my upbringing. I was fortunate to have been raised by my mother—a clinical psychologist and the epitome of a Quetzal Mama. During the 1970s, my mother began practicing a form of philosophy referred to as "Creative Dynamics." The Creative Dynamics movement of the 1970s was rooted in positive thinking, tapped into the power of the mind/body connection, and outlined how positive thinking and visualization attract positive outcomes. Some of the key tenets of Creative Dynamics included goal setting, visualization, power of language, and the law of attraction. My mother's bible was Jonathan Livingston Seagull (Richard Bach), and my siblings and I were her disciples. In my room, she placed a poster above my bed that read, "If You Can Dream It, You Can Become It." She taught us that words were powerful and advised us to be cautious of our language. For example, in our home we could not use the phrase, "I can't." She believed the negative contraction "can't" was a self- fulfilling phenomena. She would ask us instead to use the term "challenge" when we encountered something that seemed out of our abilities.

All of this may sound like 1970s self-help mumbo jumbo, but all of my siblings are very successful persons. Among the four of us, we have attended Harvard, Stanford, University of Chicago, Santa Clara University, UC Berkeley, UC San Diego, and University of Wisconsin. Fortunately, with the lessons we learned from our mother, we have passed this down to our own children.

While my mom was practicing Creative Dynamics, my father's parental philosophy could be summed up by his favorite phrase: "This aint' no damn hotel!" His style was more regimented and structured—possibly from his service as a Seabee in the Navy. He believed in being task oriented, earning your keep (so to speak), being the strongest link in the chain, and striving to the best of your abilities academically. He wanted us to appreciate that everything he had he earned and that life was not about entitlements. He referred to the television as "The Idiot Box" and told us everything we needed to know could be found in a book. All of us were constant readers, no doubt. We had to rise early, be productive, and go to school or work. There were no other options. Oh yeah—and you'd better get straight A's!

He felt fear was the greatest motivator and that negative reinforcement worked best. When I think of my father's parenting style, I think of Chris Farley's character on *Saturday Night Live* – the "Motivational Speaker." This is a hilarious rendition of my father's negative reinforcement style. Farley's mantra of "living in a van down by the river" is similar to my dad's motivational style. A "rude awakening" was always lurking around the corner if we did not follow his wisdom.

Aside from his fear tactics and negative reinforcement, my dad has always been very astute politically. He is someone who can see the bigger picture and appreciates how complex factors shape and influence our world. For example, he often discussed domestic and world political structures and the differences between those with and without power. He schooled us in the reality of the power structure known as "the man" and how this symbolic entity affects the lives of Latinos. From my dad, I learned some valuable lessons that I passed along to my children:

- Nothing in life is free (hence, "This aint no damn hotel").
- There is always someone smarter, faster, and better than you.
- Vote in every election. It matters.

And the most important advice: Those with the highest academic achievements will get the biggest piece of cheese.

Having been raised by these two dramatically contrasting parenting styles, I was able to identify the style I adapted for my own children. My style, and what I believe is an extremely effective parenting method, is outlined in this book.

One absolute fact emerged as I outlined the definitive strategies for college preparation. That fact is that the strategies cannot be effective without the philosophy that guides them. The reverse is also true: The philosophy cannot work in isolation without the strategies. I knew from my own work in raising my children that my guiding philosophy had the greatest impact on my children's eventual success.

This book focuses exclusively on academic success. While there are other ways in which Latino children can demonstrate ability, the reality is your child's academic success has the greatest impact on his/her future overall success in *any* endeavor. For this reason, I choose to focus on academic success for Latino children.

This book is strategically segmented into three parts. Part One focuses on the 10 Quetzal Mama Principles – the guiding philosophy that prepares the psychological foundation. Part Two teaches parents how to "Work the System" and provides key terms, resources, and timelines to map out your child's academic strategy. Finally, Part Three contains the "nitty gritty" college admission instructions, tips, and secrets to help your child get into the best college or university possible.

All three parts are essential for your child's academic success and can be read in any order you choose. However, it is recommended you read and implement the 10 Quetzal Mama Principles first because they set the foundation for everything else. In order to implement many of the rigorous strategies successfully that I have outlined in Part Two, you will need to have your children already "on board," so to speak.

Throughout the book, you will see references to some of the most competitive and highly ranked universities (Harvard, Yale, Princeton, etc.). I refer to these prestigious institutions as a point of reference, intending to inspire and to establish a higher benchmark. I do not refer to these institutions to alienate or to discourage readers who may not identify with this level of achievement. I wrote this book with the conviction that parents will use the tools and methods outlined to help their student in *any* academic endeavor—whether that includes an AA degree, vocational or trade school, or a public or private college.

I also wrote this book because I am very concerned about the state of our public schools–mostly, the opportunity gap between whites/Asians and Latinos, African Americans, and Native American students. Our children of color are falling behind. By the time one of our "lucky" brown students happens to grab the attention of a high school counselor, it is often too late. I am not blaming high school counselors. What I am saying is if a student begins to strategize a path to college in high school, it is often too late. As Quetzal Mamas we cannot wait around or rely on others to strategize and establish the academic path of our children. We must take charge and do it ourselves.

As Latinos, we are a people of extreme resilience. We are tireless, smart, and do not cut corners. True to our spirit, lets focus on how we can overcome challenges and not on how they are preventing us from moving ahead.

Yes, it is easier to sit back and blame others for our failures. We can blame the public school system, institutionalized racism, our socioeconomic status, our lack of resources, or a myriad of excuses. I am not saying these factors do not exist, nor am I saying they do not negatively alter or impact our children's opportunities. Trust me. I know these barriers; my children know these barriers; and the previous generations before me can attest to these painful barriers.

What I am saying is that although these barriers exist, we can accept them and concede defeat; or we can become Quetzal warriors and build a plan around them. I wrote this book with the conviction that Quetzal Mamas and Papas can work around these barriers, and our children will succeed despite them.

I challenge Latino parents to apply tools from every chapter in this book. Or, do as other parents have done by creating Quetzal Mama Café's throughout the U.S. These cafes are popping up in towns like Milwaukee, Wisconsin, Oakdale, California, and San Antonio, Texas. Parents are taking chapters from this book and holding their own discussion groups to implement the strategies for their families.

If you are reading this book and have exciting information to share with other Quetzal Mamas or Papas, or have used these tools with success, share your story at quetzalmama@gmail.com.

I challenge you to become a Quetzal Mama.

Roxanne Ocampo
Quetzal Mama and mother of three thriving, ambitious, driven, successful, humble, and kind children

PART ONE

THE QUETZAL MAMA PHILOSOPHY

PART ONE DEFINES a Quetzal Mama, and focuses on the philosophy of raising Latino superstars – including the 10 Quetzal Mama Principles, and a review of myths that may sabotage efforts in raising superstars.

CHAPTER 1

WHAT IS A QUETZAL MAMA?

WHAT IS A Quetzal Mama? You might know a couple of them. If you are reading this book, you are probably one of them. I am a Quetzal Mama, my sisters are Quetzal Mamas, and my mom and mother-in-law are both Quetzal Mamas. Pronounced "ket-sal," a Quetzal Mama is a proud Latina mom who will do anything to ensure her children fulfill their chosen path. A Quetzal Mama knows her children have unique gifts and talents and will make a profound contribution to society. As such, a Quetzal Mama provides her children with every opportunity for success; and removes all barriers.

The term Quetzal Mama came to me when I was trying to pinpoint and name the rearing method I practiced with my children. The term "mama" is universal. A Quetzal Mama can be a father, *abuelito*, godparent, stepparent, *tia* or *tio*, or any person who takes an active role in guiding a student's academic journey.

As a feminist, it is important that my readers do not misinterpret this powerful label. I am not perpetuating a sexist stereotype, nor am I declaring that males are inadequate bystanders in the child rearing process. There are many fathers who take their parental role seriously and are fully engaged in the process of raising successful children (my husband and brothers-in-law are examples). If you are the person in a child's life who has the inclination, organizational skills, tenacity, passion, and long-term commitment required to pull off the enormous task of academic guidance, then you are a Quetzal Mama.

The term, "Quetzal Mama," arose when I read Amy Chua's, *The Battle Hymn of the Tiger Mother*—a book marketed as an Asian parents' child-rearing philosophy. I felt Latino families needed a positive brand or label to represent our critical and positive role in rearing our children.

I chose the name "Quetzal" because of the powerful imagery and history associated with this species of bird. The quetzal bird is a symbol of freedom and liberty and played an important role in indigenous mythology. The word "Quetzal" is Nahuatl (Aztec). The root *Quetz* means "stand" derived from *Quetzalli*, and refers to a "tall, upstanding plume."

The Mayans considered the male tail feathers of the Quetzal worth more than gold, and their plumes could only be adorned by Mayan priests or nobility as a symbol of authority. The Aztec deity Quetzalcoatl (the "Plumed Serpent") was worshipped by the Aztecs.

Interestingly, the quetzal bird cannot survive in captivity and is known to kill itself after being caged or captured. For this reason, I chose the quetzal bird to be a symbol of liberty for Latino students. We are a beautiful species but were made captive by the European colonizers. We have been imprisoned by stereotypes, discrimination, and internalized racism. We have, in a sense, been captive since 1492.

Thankfully, a new awakening is occurring. Quetzals are coming out of their cages and taking their rightful place in their adapted habitat. Listen quietly. You will hear the rusty cage doors clanking while the tonal flight sounds of the Quetzal pervade the air! I challenge you to break out of your cage and become a Quetzal Mama.

CHAPTER 2

THE QUETZAL MAMA PHILOSOPHY

THE QUETZAL MAMA philosophy is based on two premises: parental involvement and high expectations. The single, most fundamental concept that has the greatest impact in helping your child succeed starts with you: *the parent.* Your role starts at the beginning of your child's academic career and continues until the day they walk across the platform receiving their college diploma. Do not underestimate the role you play in this process. Without your part, it is highly unlikely your child will succeed. And, do not underestimate how the concept of high expectations will impact your child's life. Setting high expectations early and reinforcing these standards consistently is instrumental to your child's success.

My husband and I followed the 10 Quetzal Mama Principles in raising our three children. Each child has unique talents, gifts, and a personality disposition independent of each other. However, all three know they have a higher purpose in life, are working hard to fulfill their contribution to humanity, and have confidence they will succeed. All three children have great respect for each other and honor their special place in our family. All three children have an apparent drive and attitude that sets them apart.

Some of you reading these comments may already be thinking, "Sure, her children are succeeding because they all share the same DNA!" I will admit my children are smart. However, smartness does not make a driven, high achieving student. Furthermore, intelligence

5

does not necessarily yield a child with empathy, compassion, or the desire to serve humanity. There are many students with exceptional IQs, who remain unmotivated, uninspired, and unproductive. I believe the difference that separates my children from other smart children, is the Quetzal Mama philosophy.

So what is the Quetzal Mama philosophy? It is my theory of how (and why) your children can thrive and succeed in elementary, middle, high school, and college. It is based on the belief your child has a greater purpose in life, is obligated to fulfill that purpose, and that you will do everything possible for your child to realize this purpose.

This theory is so simple, so easy, and so natural, you may not believe it. You may ask, "If this is so easy, then why don't all parents do this?" I ask myself this same question every day.

The Quetzal Mama philosophy is relative – it means every Latino child can achieve greatness at a relative level. Whether your child is intellectually gifted, above average, average, or struggles in school, his/her achievement via the Quetzal Mama philosophy is relative to the child's respective starting point. This is an important concept to grasp because every child has different capabilities and unique gifts. Therefore, every Latino child will yield different and unique results—each as wonderful as any other.

The Quetzal Mama philosophy is unique to Latino culture and unique in the philosophy of why our children *should* succeed. The critical factor that makes this principle different from other philosophies lies within the modal verb "should" versus "must." Let me explain.

Consider the book, *Battle Hymn of the Tiger Mother*, a book I referenced in the previous chapter. The Tiger Mom philosophy claims to be an Asian construct: you *must* be ultra competitive; you *must* succeed at any and every expense; you *must* be Number One and outperform your peers; etc.

The Quetzal Mama philosophy differs from the Tiger Mom philosophy in that Latino children *should* perform at the best of their abilities and *should* push themselves for greatness, but for a very different set of reasons. The Tiger Mom philosophy advocates a "must" mandate; and the reasons for this "must" rest within the individual, with success being exclusive to that individual. For example, students who follow the Tiger Mom philosophy *must* be Number One—not so they can give back to humanity or to help others, but to get to the top (whatever and wherever that is) for status and prestige. It makes the concept of challenge an actual goal. It is about individual winnings and individual success. Win, win, win. It is a "me" win, not an "us" win. It is about succeeding for the sake of competitiveness, for the family name, for social status, for the medal, all focusing and serving the individual.

On the other hand, the modal verb *should* represents the expectation we hold for our Latino children. The Quetzal Mama philosophy rests on the belief your children have unique gifts and talents that *should* be used toward the betterment of humanity. Any child who has been told his or her talents will be used to help others; to provide a breakthrough in a particular discipline; or to change how the world looks, feels, or thinks, will feel empowered. This is a much different outlook than believing his/her gifts will be used to become Number One, obtain the highest SAT score, or outperform his or her classmates—for the mere sake of outperforming them.

I do agree, *to a very limited extent*, with the Tiger Mom child-rearing style. I agree with being a strict parent, pushing your child to perform at his/her ability, encouraging your child to strive to be the "best" in all endeavors, and reinforcing the principle that school work is priority.

Interestingly, *both* Tiger Mom's daughter and Quetzal Mama's daughter walked Harvard University's commencement in spring 2015.

However, for the reasons stated above, I do not agree with the *motivation* that drives this type of parent. In my opinion, the quality of life is higher and more fulfilling for the child raised by the Quetzal Mama philosophy versus the Tiger Mom philosophy. While a child raised by the Quetzal Mama philosophy is empowered in his/her educational pursuits and life goals, a child raised by a Tiger Mom is forced to follow a rigid, pre-defined, academic and career path.

The child raised by the Quetzal Mama philosophy knows his/her path is righteous and is confident of success. The child will not focus on "beating" anyone and, instead, focus on challenging him/herself to fulfill a path in life. This child knows s/he is destined to contribute to humanity in a profound way and knows high academic accomplishments will serve the community. The child focuses on a higher goal—rather than focusing on "beating" anyone.

At the end of the journey, children raised by the Tiger Mom philosophy will be endlessly chasing a dangling carrot, while the children raised by the Quetzal Mama philosophy will have already taken flight and will be soaring.

Gabriella R. Herrera, Valedictorian 2011
(Daughter of Quetzal Mama)
Merrill F. West High School, Tracy, California
Begins Harvard Medical School Fall 2016 with
the goal to serve her community
Photo by Glenn Moore/Tracy Press 2011

CHAPTER 3

THE 10 QUETZAL MAMA PRINCIPLES

THE QUETZAL MAMA philosophy embraces 10 Quetzal Mama Principles. All of the 10 principles have the following commonalities. First, all 10 fall under the general philosophical tenet of *high expectations*. Second, all 10 must be practiced consistently and repetitively. Consistent and repetitive messaging will make the difference between little, marginal, or great success.

Before you read the 10 Quetzal Mama Principles, remember the old expression, "More is caught than taught." If you are setting expectations for your children, but you (or your spouse) are not behaving in ways that demonstrate and support these ideals, then you are simply lecturing. To borrow another expression, you are "talking the talk, but not walking the walk." Or, as we say in Spanish, "*Del dicho al hecho ay mucho trecho.*" All of your hard work in implementing the 10 Quetzal Mama Principles will not be effective if you only verbalize expectations but do not personally demonstrate behaviors.

Both my parents and my husband's parents voluntarily served within their respective Latino communities *for several decades*. We grew up watching our parents' behaviors and "catching" them in action. Naturally, my husband and I volunteer our time and services in our community. This is how we "walk the walk." Just as Arturo and I witnessed our own parents serving their communities, our children have grown up witnessing how we sacrificed our time, money, and energies to help Latino students and families within our community. It is no coincidence our children are now engaging in community service within their respective college communities. To be successful in implementing the 10 Quetzal Mama Principles, remember to "walk the walk."

The following 10 principles are not organized in order of importance or application. These principles can be implemented individually or concurrently. Some parents may adopt one or two principles that resonate with their personality or parenting style, while other parents will want to embrace fully all 10 principles.

Quetzal Mama Principle #1

You (the parent) realize and appreciate the power and responsibility you possess for the direction of your child's academic future.
Your belief, involvement, and actions will have the greatest impact on your child's life than all other stimulus combined.

The *Hispanic Journal of Behavioral Sciences* published the paper entitled, *From Barrios to Yale: The Role of Parenting Strategies in Latino Families.* This paper was written by Dr. Ceballo, a psychology professor at the University of Michigan, who examined Latino student scholarly achievement at Yale University. One of the primary characteristics Ceballo identified was *a strong parental commitment to the importance of education.* Ceballo noted, "All of the students portrayed their parents as maintaining an almost unconditional commitment to education." Similarly, many other researchers have arrived at the same conclusion regarding Latino academic success: The higher the parental involvement, the higher the student's academic success.

Take a moment to digest this. This principle focuses on your parental responsibility for controlling your child's future and takes the power away from factors you cannot control (like school systems, teachers, institutions, etc.). When you realize the power you have to control your child's destiny, it will be a liberating experience. Your parental commitment will have a direct impact on your child, your grandchildren, and your great grandchildren.

QUETZAL MAMA PRINCIPLE #2

Your child has a higher purpose in life that must be realized.
Today, this very moment, clearly state to your child, in a matter-of-fact way, that s/he has a gift, a purpose, a higher goal or mission, that must be accomplished. Yes – I mean *literally* tell your child that s/he is chosen and has a purpose.

Your child will naturally ask you, "How do you know this?" Answer as truthfully as possible. It is not so important *how* you came to this realization but that you believe it and that you defend your position with absolute conviction.

Now you will ask me, "How *did* I know this?" The simple answer is that you realized this a long time ago but may not have articulated it. It may not have even registered in your mind on a conscious level, but you know. The fact you are reading this book and came to this item confirms your belief. It could be something you felt when you were expecting your child, a dream you had, a religious experience, people's constant praise or recognition of your child's talents, comments from your child's teacher, or something you see in your child.

Take time to envision how and where you will share this momentous declaration with your child. Your credibility will be scrutinized, so you will seriously need to consider the delivery of your message. I would recommend rehearsing this with your spouse or a friend. On the other hand, this cannot be an obviously rehearsed or forced statement. It should seem natural—as if you were telling your child s/he has brown hair (a fact, something you are just declaring). You will repeat this, in various ways, throughout your child's lifetime; so do not be overdramatic or over rehearsed. When something comes from the heart, it is usually delivered perfectly and does not require practice. It should be as if you had a secret you just decided was the right time to share with your child.

Bottom line – it is our responsibility as parents to validate our children's special gift to humanity. If we don't validate them, who will? Don't assume your child knows s/he has special talents or gifts. Even if you feel you've indirectly communicated this belief to your child, you must tell them, literally.

Quetzal Mama Principle #3
Clean house, literally.
Principle #3 is something to which most parents can easily relate. Most of us are employed in some capacity, so we work every day with different types of people with different personalities and dispositions. There is usually someone in everyone's workplace with a personality disposition I refer to as "Negative Nelly." This is the person whose mantra is, "It'll never work." These types of people are always suspect of persons with a positive attitude and optimistic outlook. If you bring Negative Nelly freshly baked cookies, she will tell you how many calories are in them. If you tell her you want to send your daughter to an Ivy League school, she will roll her eyes at the financial "burden." Quetzal Mamas stay away from Negative Nellys and make sure their children are protected from them as well.

If your child's environment is polluted with nay-sayers, pessimists, and Negative Nellys who don't understand or appreciate the concept of a higher purpose, get rid of them! Your home is your child's sanctuary, and this space is where nearly all of your work will be conducted. This space must be filled with positive inspiration.

You cannot control 100 percent of the comments, suggestions, or positive or negative feedback your child will encounter on any given day. However, you can control what is communicated to your child within your own household. Make this your priority.

In the work environment example, we are not afforded the luxury of controlling the personality types in our workplace. However, your home is controlled by you. Create an environment with images that empower and reinforce your child's destiny.

Some examples of how you can change the environment include adorning your child's bedroom walls with visual images that support your belief in their higher purpose. Posters I have had in my children's bedrooms include César Chávez; Ché Guevarra; Mahatma Ghandi; and Martin Luther King, Jr. We also had photographs of Astronaut Ellen Ochoa and Astronaut José Hernandez. My three children also have had pennants and other images from Ivy League universities, as well as their awards from elementary through high school.

The constant visual message should be, "You can; you should; they did." These will be the images they see when they wake up in the morning, and the last images they see before they go to sleep.

Along the lines of cleaning house, watching and monitoring the types of students with whom your child interacts is also important. Pay credence to the saying, "Birds of a feather flock together." Surround your child with students who are also on a path toward academic success and whose parents share similar philosophical ideals.

The next step moves you away from the philosophical and theoretical into a behavioral aspect of the Quetzal Mama Principle.

Quetzal Mama Principle #4

Behave in ways that support your belief in your child's higher purpose.

You have a child who will be contributing in a profound way to mankind. Knowing this fact will compel you to act and to behave in certain ways around your child. When you know with conviction your child is destined for greatness, you will begin to behave in ways that support this.

One example of behaving in ways to support your belief is to be your child's public relations officer, marketing strategist, and inspirational guru. Yes, you will "market" your child because his/her talents must be broadcast to provide visual reinforcement as well as to attest to your child's special talents.

When my children excelled at a sport, art, or academic pursuit, I would take a digital photo of them, write up a caption, and email it to the appropriate section editor of our local newspaper. Or, I would post it on my social media page. This sounds crazy to Latino parents! Our culture has taught us it is inappropriate to brag, to boast, and to assertively publicize our child's accomplishments.

But, we need to get over this. If you are not advocating for your child in every medium possible, who will do it for them? It is wonderful to watch your child's reaction when s/he finds the newspaper on the kitchen table with a photo and write-up! This is a free, relatively easy, but powerful tool you can use to emphasize the importance of your Latino child. If you are unsure to whom to send this information, go online and look up your local newspaper. Most newspapers have the names and email addresses of editors for each section. If you do not have a local newspaper, contact your local County Office of Education (they usually produce a quarterly newsletter), or contact your child's school newspaper.

Another example of taking steps to show your belief in your child's higher purpose is to participate in activities that support long-term goals. For example, if your son or daughter enters a spelling bee, have the entire family pitch in to demonstrate support. For example, take turns practicing words, engage in quizzes, or help research the etymology of particular words. Your participation will demonstrate your belief in your daughter or son's abilities.

Another example might be enrolling your child in activities consistent with his/her educational or career goals. If Maribel is interested in marine biology, enroll her in a summer camp dealing with science; or have her participate in a local or county science fair. In addition, you might buy her books on the subject and take her to hear lectures by local marine biologists (or watch videos online).

Similarly, if Juan is interested in political science, take him to the State Capitol, or make an appointment to have him personally meet his congressional representative. If a political event is occurring in your region, take Juan to witness the live event.

These are just a few examples of how your behavior can reinforce your belief in your child's higher purpose. Ideally, you will find *Latino* role models while engaging your children in this process.

While Principle #3 described behaviors to express your belief in your child's higher purpose, the next principle focuses on language.

Quetzal Mama Principle #5
Language is powerful.
Choose language that encourages, enlightens, and inspires your child. While visual imagery and behavioral aspects are very important in

following the Quetzal Mama Principles, the use of language is also a critical tool. Words have a definite energy associated with them. To understand my point, stand in front of your mirror and try to say the words, "pathetic" or "traumatic." Next, say the words, "love" or "happiness." The energy in your space will change, as will the natural facial expressions that occur when you mouth these words. Notice the differences, and consider the impact powerful and inspirational words can have in your child's life.

Be mindful of the use of negative language. For example, rather than using words such as "can't" or "impossible," consider framing the situation with the term, "challenge." Be mindful as well as to the way we may insult or negatively criticize our children. Instead, focus on how their behaviors might not serve them well—so as to focus on the *behavior* versus attacking the *person*. When we see our children faltering in some area, give them examples of choices or options that can help them succeed.

Remember, as adults we have the privilege and experience of having survived our mistakes. Give your children the power to make mistakes, but also give them options to help correct their mistakes. Focus on the behavior, and steer clear of negative language that will leave them feeling demoralized and defeated.

Children do understand the concept that all people are good, but sometimes we make bad decisions. It is empowering for a child to feel in control of his/her destiny, based on their actions. This is a completely different experience than telling your child, "You will never be successful because . . ."

Another example of the power of language can be found in "labels." We Latinos are notoriously crafty and giving nicknames (aka labels) – Techo or Two-Story, Shark, Clam. I love this part of our culture.

Unfortunately, many of these labels may be interpreted as negative. When parents use negative language or labels, it has the potential for long-lasting and negative outcomes. For example, labels like "Flojo" or "Tonta" have obvious negative connotations. When children hear repetitive negative language from a person of authority, they often internalize these labels and live up to the negative expectations.

Instead, use this psychological tool to reverse the outcome. Use positive labels to identify your child like "smart," "brilliant," "curious," or "scientific." If you use these words repetitively, your child will begin to behave in ways consistent with the label. Remember, the foundation of the Quetzal Mama philosophy is high expectations. Use words that emphasize your high expectations.

In addition to using positive versus negative language, consider how grammatical components of language can also impact your child's future success. Speak from a position of absolute expectation. Eliminate words such as "if" and replace with "when." For example, "*When* you begin your freshman year in college, it is likely you will live on campus."

The subordinating conjunction "when" indicates a specific place and time and indicates an absolute expectation. Your child will come to view your high expectation (from "when") as a normal and given part of his/her life. Whether consciously or subconsciously, your child will pursue that which is expected.

On the other hand, when we hear the subordinating conjunction "if," it automatically indicates existence of doubt and/or potential for failure. Note how a simple part of our language can significantly impact how your child views him/herself. Consider the words of President Barack Obama:

> "If you quit on school,
> you're not only quitting on yourself,
> you're quitting on your country."

This is an example of how the conjunction "if" presumes failure as a possibility. Instead, replace "if" with "when" to create the following *positive* statement:

> When you win in school,
> it's a win for our country.

The above example illustrates how a single word completely changes the impact of the message. A more practical example arises when I present student workshops regarding the Personal Statement and scholarship essays. I ask students to replace one set of common phrases with an ideal set of phrases:

I hope to . . .I will
I think I might . . .I intend to
I would like to . . .I will pursue

The next component is quintessential Quetzal Mama because it has to do with our *cultura*.

QUETZAL MAMA PRINCIPLE #6
Authenticate and value your child's Latino identity.
As the wise César Chávez said, "*We need to help students and parents cherish and preserve the ethnic and cultural diversity that nourishes and strengthens this community—and this nation.*" Cesar knew. It is our responsibility to educate our children regarding our proud heritage and why our heritage has value.

When I say "authenticate and value your child's Latino identity," I am referring to an enculturation process that begins in your home. This enculturation process is intended to help your child develop pride in being Latino. This process should include discussions about our historical and cultural figures, politics, exposing your children *our students* to books about Latinos, and celebrating and educating your children *our students* about our unique traditions. Basically, teach your children to feel proud to be Latino!

I always knew there was a direct correlation between Latino students who are proud of their heritage and their academic success. I have witnessed this phenomena at academic achievement events such as "Latino Graduation" or Latino Scholarship and Recognition Award events. Research indicates a direct correlation between Latino students with the highest level of positive cultural identity and academic success.

Rather than citing various studies, you should know that, in general, researchers have found positive ethnic (Latino) identity is associated with higher academic achievement, higher self-esteem, resilience, and graduation from college.

If you want to see this phenomenon in full effect, attend a Latino-themed graduation commencement in your community. You will see – as I have repeatedly – that the proud Latino students attending these events will invariably have strong GPA's, exceptional service within their communities, and are on track to begin their undergraduate or graduate studies. And, in the audience you will see hundreds of Quetzal Mamas and Papas.

Unfortunately, in our society, Latinos (and especially Mexican Americans) have been taught, in direct and indirect ways, that we are not as appreciated as other ethnic groups. Although we are nearly 50 percent of the population in California, we are rarely depicted positively in the media (with the exception of a prostitute, gang-banger, or criminal), we are underrepresented in academia (especially within the STEM fields), and our children currently have the lowest college degree holding rates of all racial/ethnic groups in the U.S.

What I just said is not news to Latino parents. I make this point to emphasize the importance of elevating your child's perception of him/herself amidst the constant flow of negative information pervasive in the classroom, on the playground, and in the media.

Instead of fruitlessly trying to adapt and assimilate into the dominant culture, naively believing it will somehow help your child succeed, be proud of who you are and what you can contribute to our great country. After all, isn't that one of the principles that made this country the best place on earth?

So what are the types of things you can do to instill ethnic pride in your child? First, you need to know your roots. Malcolm X said it best: *"You have to have a knowledge of history no matter what you are going to do; anything that you undertake you have to have a knowledge of history in order to be successful in it."*

As Latinos, we have an incredible history. Unfortunately, our children are not told about our history in school or through the media. Therefore, it is your job to educate your child about our rich history.

If you have not been exposed to our history, there are many things you can do. Ideally, you will do these activities with your child so that s/he will learn along with you. It is not a difficult task, and you will enjoy the learning experience. This can be a very inexpensive activity, if not free.

Begin with researching pre-Columbian history in the Americas—be it Mayan, Aztec, or any other indigenous group to which you feel connected. The particular Indian nation or indigenous culture is not as important as the message that we descend from civilizations that had advanced knowledge and resources long before Europeans set foot on their territory.

For example, our daughter who intends to be a neurosurgeon, was delighted to learn our pre-Columbian ancestors conducted a form of brain surgery (called trepanation) nearly 3,000 years ago. The evidence was found in archeological sites where craniums were discovered with healed and fused craniums post-surgery. This means a hole was drilled into their cranium, and the patient survived the surgery long enough for the cranium to have re-grown and fused. You can find other relevant evidence to show your children how advanced our civilizations were before the Europeans colonized.

In addition to the historical framework of your ethnic roots, you should also know your actual ancestral roots. Teaching your children exactly where they came from and how they arrived here is a powerful experience.

You might consider genealogical research (as a family) to discover historical facts about your ancestry. In addition to learning about the migratory path of your ancestors, you will soon realize and appreciate the hardships and obstacles your ancestors made that resulted in where you and your children are standing today (literally and figuratively).

Encourage your children to share their newly acquired information with their teachers—as a way to enlighten their classmates as well as correct historical non-facts.

For example, when our son Emilio was eight years old, he was learning about the "pioneers" in California (as part of the California Content Standard "History-Social Science"). He corrected his teacher by citing the names of the indigenous tribes who were already living in the same location before the "pioneers" arrived. When his class project was to build a log cabin, he built a tee pee (with a planted squash and corn garden) next to the cabin to pay tribute to the indigenous people he learned about from his own research.

As an extension of his contribution in educating his teacher about factual California history, he chose to follow the example of his brother Carlos, and dressed up as an indigenous person during the week his classmates dressed as "pioneers." He was the only student in his school to dress up as an indigenous person, but he did so with pride. His dress represented his symbolic homage to all the indigenous persons who have been forgotten and served as a walking class project, so to speak.

In fourth grade, Emilio was required to complete a California mission project. Instead of writing a report about how benevolent Spanish priests "enlightened" the "savage" Indians, he instead asked his older brother to help him film a video about the Chumash Indians. In the filmed video, Emilio addressed how the Chumash Indians revolted against the harsh mistreatment of the priests. He posted the video on YouTube.

Emilio Ocampo, Eight Years Old, Hirsch Elementary School
Educating his teacher and classmates about the
contributions of Native Americans

Carlos Ocampo, Fourth Grade, Eight Years Old
Representing a tribal chief as part of "Pioneer Days"

Quetzal Mama Principle #7

Focus on non-academic activities.

Expose your child to the arts. Your child, from infancy, should be constantly exposed to beautiful sounds of music, visual art, textiles, and even food art. You will want your child to experience all that is in our small world, not just the daily in-and-out lives of school and home. Experiencing the arts is truly an experience in travel. And it is a travel experience that will not cost you a penny! Fortunately, with the Internet and public libraries, you can expose your child to artwork, listen to sounds of jazz musicians, and read historical biographies of famous contributors to the arts.

For example, see the talented muralist Judith Francisca Baca by visiting her website; or show your children examples of *Los Tres Grandes* muralists (Diego Rivera, José Orozco, and David Siqueiros). If you Google "Mexican sculptors," you will find a list of at least 100 artists.

Each time you view a particular work, you should use it as a cultural and historical learning experience. Not only will your children have a greater understanding of their culture, but also they will have knowledge most students have not had the privilege of experiencing.

To identify famous Latino composers, sit with your child as you Google some of these famous Mexican composers. Listen to a sample of the incredible works of Daniel Catán, Agustín Lara, Carlos Chávez, Gabriela Ortiz, Manuel Ponce, or Silvestre Revueltas.

Because Latinos are also gifted in literary arts, you will have a myriad of written works for your child to read. Go to your library and check out some of the works by Gabriel García Márquez, Isabel Allende, Victor Villaseñor, or the poetry of Pablo Neruda. These are only a few. If you

Google famous Latino authors, you can view their titles and consider their particular style of writing.

This exploration of the arts can be a lifelong journey, and it should be shared by your entire family.

A sub-set of this principle of exposing your child to the arts is to begin musical training as early as possible. Reading and playing music, as well as listening to music, is fundamental to your child's academic growth, specifically enhancing mathematic abilities.

We do not need to understand the complexities of the corpus callosum or occipital lobe to grasp this concept. We have all heard about the "Mozart effect" – the research that suggests that exposing your child to classical music before the age of seven impacts the child's mathematical performance. This research suggests the pitch, rhythm, and musical compositions sequential in nature help your child with mathematic abilities. The theory is that classical music targets a specific area of our brain that stimulates temporal reasoning (useful in mathematical functions).

Listening to classical music is not enough. Your child should begin musical training at the earliest age possible. Musical training is a highly complex function that requires the brain to process sound (temporal lobe), mimic sound through manual expression (posterior parietal cortex), and to process visual stimulus (sheet music) through the occipital lobe. All three of our children read music and play musical instruments. Emilio plays the piano and xylophone; Gabi plays the violin and cello; and Carlos plays the drums.

If you are skeptical about the correlation between musical training and academic achievement, I encourage you to identify research findings on this topic that have been completed by leading neurobiologists. Better yet, attend your district's annual music festival (if you have one). If you do not have one, visit your local city youth orchestra. Talk with the parents of these musicians, and ask them about their children's academic background. These students tend to be in the top 10 percent of their school and are extremely motivated to perform well academically. Is it the chicken or the egg? Did these students gravitate toward music because their brain is wired differently, or did their brain develop differently because they were exposed to music? I don't know, but I'm keeping Emilio in piano lessons as long as I can!

Emilio Ocampo, Third Grade Piano Recital

Along the lines of exposing your children to various forms of music, encourage your children to listen to *corridos*. Our Latino history is rich with *corridos*—a powerful narrative song that represents the social and political history of Latinos.

Quetzal Mama Principle #8
Establish unique family rituals
You do not have to follow transcendental psychology to believe in the power of ritual. If you interview the leader of any successful team—whether

an NFL Super Bowl coach, the CEO of a Fortune 100 company, or the President of the United States—you will learn that ritual is a highly effective incentive practiced among successful groups.

Every society from ancient to the present has engaged in rituals through some form. In the NFL example, a ritual can be a moment of reflection prior to the game. In the CEO example, a ritual can be a pre-product launch ceremony. In the Presidential example, a ritual can be the State of the Union Address. All of these examples illustrate how humans have a need to form a collective spiritual union, engage in a contemplative moment, and share their collective positive energies toward a singular goal.

Ritual is an effective reinforcement and motivational tool because it allows us to tap into our meditative state and focus our positive energy toward a particular goal. And, because children thrive on repetition and structure, ritual is also a great parenting tool.

Ritual can assume many forms. It can be words written on a paper, a physical activity, a prayer, or any number of things. For example, throughout my children's elementary and secondary education, I would say the following six words as I pulled into the school roundabout each morning: "*Show 'em what you're made of.*" Interestingly, on the rare occasion when I forgot to tell them, they would say, "Mom, you forgot to tell us to show them what we're made of!" I would then tell them, and they'd confidently and happily be off to school.

This powerful statement was the last words of advice before my kids began their school day. In that simple statement, I was reaffirming they are talented, smart, and powerful individuals. It is their duty to ensure they live up to their abilities.

Another family ritual we've participated in for more than 10 years is a circle of prayer. When anyone in our family is focused on a particular goal or enduring a particular challenge, our entire family joins together

29

to form a prayer circle. As part of our ritual we light the end of braided sweet grass – a gift by a tribal elder, braided during an Indian ceremony in South Dakota in spring 2005. We hold hands and pray silently. When Carlos and Gabi left home for college, Arturo cut a piece of this same sweet grass and ceremonially placed it in a small wooden box. Our children kept their box in their dorm rooms throughout college.

Your ritual can be anything you wish it to be, as long as it is authentic to your family and has meaning. The key is to be committed to engaging in your family ritual in a consistent manner.

QUETZAL MAMA PRINCIPLE #9

Help your child develop a positive mindset and self-affirmation strategies.

So far, most of the Quetzal Mama principles are strategies implemented exclusively by the parent. Principle #9 is different because it requires participation by your child(ren).

Positive Mindset and Self-Affirmation are two independent concepts, but I have included them together because they go hand-in-hand. I will discuss them separately so that you can appreciate their unique value.

Positive Mindset. Unlike other tangible things we can see, hear, or touch, a positive mindset requires faith and willpower. When I asked the renowned brain surgeon Dr. Alfredo Quinones-Hinojosa his thoughts on positive mindset to impact change, he said: "If you can believe beyond what your eyes can see and enjoy the thumping of your heart against your chest like a jack hammer from excitement in a dream, then your brain can definitely achieve it!"

One of the most powerful life strategies is to develop a positive mindset. Using positive thinking techniques, self-affirmations and visualization, may be instrumental in achieving your life goals. This sounds hokey, I know. Before you dismiss this important concept, I challenge you to try the techniques outlined in this chapter.

Since our children were very young, we talked with each child about using their most powerful weapon: their mind. Our children have grown to respect and to value how a positive mindset can help them in all of their endeavors. Focusing on positive energy, positive opportunities, and positive outcomes is a powerful way to control our responses to life events. When we choose to focus on positive energy and positive outcomes, we exert control over our life situations. This is far more powerful than accepting status quo, negative outcomes, or "life's hand."

A positive mindset does not happen overnight. Developing a positive mindset is a fluid process that requires on-going exercises. Helping your child develop a positive mindset is truly a lifelong process. It begins the moment your child can sense your own energy and continues through their formative years, high school, college, and beyond. A positive mindset is like a tree: It is cultivated, rooted, and eventually blossoms.

It is far easier to succumb to negative thinking because it requires far less work! It allows for casting blame on others, ignoring personal responsibility, and conceding "fate." Negative thinkers assume no accountability for their life position or for their children's life positions. They do not believe they can impact positive change in their life, so they refuse to accept the possibility they can impact positive change in their children's lives.

Positive thinkers, on the other hand, take charge of their life situations. They focus on how they can positively change their life situation, and how they can positively change their children's situation. Follow this principle to help your child develop and to maintain a positive mindset. In doing so, s/he will develop new thought patterns and new ways of viewing life experiences. Eventually, your child will visualize him/herself as a future scholar.

Self Affirmation. Oxford Dictionary defines self affirmation as, "The recognition and assertion of the existence and value of one's individual self." These are fancy words to say that how we view ourselves, so we are.

Self affirmation, as it relates to underrepresented students, is a psychological theory formally introduced by Dr. Claude Steele while at Stanford University in 1988. Dr. Steele is currently Executive Vice Chancellor and Provost at UC Berkeley and has served as the Dean of Education at Stanford University and previously served as Provost at Columbia University. Dr. Steele theorized people are motivated to maintain the integrity of the self, and coined the term, "stereotype threat." In a nutshell, Dr. Steele theorizes that when our social identity is attached to a negative stereotype we tend to underperform in ways that are consistent with that stereotype. His theory has particular importance for Latinos because of the negative stereotypes historically attached to our ethnic group.

Dr. Steele and his team conducted numerous studies where students were exposed to an image or verbal cue about a negative stereotype specific to their social group, prior to taking an exam or other performance event. When students are reminded of the negative stereotype prior to the event, they tend to live up to that standard. For example, if they are reminded that Latino or African-American students do not perform as well as Asian or white students on the SAT (prior to taking this exam), these students tend to underperform as expected.

Combat the concept of stereotype threat by reversing a negative suggestion with a positive one. For example, ask your child to begin a daily self-affirmation statement. Your child can say, "Today I will perform exceptionally well in science." Or, "I will score 100 percent on my math exam on Wednesday."

The point is to specify something in particular. Either imagine the positive image in your mind, say it aloud, or write it down. A combination of all three, at different times, will also be very effective.

An awesome fact is that our subconscious mind does not know whether an image we created is real or imagined. To understand what I am referring to, try the following exercise. Imagine a landscape with rays of sunlight streaming brightly onto a lake. Immediately your mind will recall and create a calm and happy physical sense of being. Your subconscious mind does not know you are only imagining this image. It will respond as though you were physically standing at that lake.

Now, use this same concept to help your children envision their future academic success. Ask your child to envision his/her name on an admissions letter from their dream college. Have your child mentally picture the words, "Welcome to the Class of 2025" on the letter. Or, ask your child to imagine italicized and embossed gold letters with his/her name on a framed diploma from their dream college. This type of positive suggestion, repeated frequently, suggests to our subconscious mind the reality of a future event.

In a study by Yale University and the University of Colorado (Geoffrey Cohen and Julio Garcia) entitled, *Recursive Processes in Self Affirmation: Intervening to Close the Minority Achievement Gap*, students of color were instructed to scribe a positive self-affirming statement on a piece of paper. This exercise was conducted in class, as a writing assignment by their teacher, and repeated throughout the school year. At the end of two years, the result was an increase in their GPA, as well as long-term positive results.

The Cohen and Garcia study illustrates how something as simple and effortless as writing a positive statement on a piece of paper can yield tremendous results. I use this strategy with the students in my Quetzal Mama Scholars Program. At the beginning of each of our coaching sessions, I ask each student to write an affirmation on a piece of paper. I do this intentionally, at the beginning of our sessions, so they can tap into the power of their subconscious mind.

Our mind is our most powerful weapon and will help us achieve positive outcomes, change our attitude, and change how we respond to life events. Pay attention to what you are thinking, what you are saying, and what images and words you allow to pervade your child's world.

Quetzal Mama Principle #10
Be large and in charge.
You are the parent, and you are in control. Assume your position of control, and you will not create a prima donna or spoiled brat.

There is a common assumption that holding high expectations for your children will create spoiled, entitled, conceited tyrants. This may be the case for parents who praise their children but do not assume their position of authority.

I saved this principle for last because it is a critical point. Growing up with a clinical psychologist as my mom, my siblings and I learned how child development is influenced by parental style. As a parent, I quickly learned that different parenting styles yield different results. To understand how parenting style affects your child's behavior, let's look at the basic parenting styles.

I would like to add a word of caution before we begin reviewing parenting styles. In approaching complex issues, I do not believe in generalities and over simplification. Generalities are just that—general guided theories to explain a particular behavior or action. When it comes to child rearing, there are many factors that shape how and why a child grows up to behave in certain ways. Child development is a complex process that must take into consideration the environment, genetics, parenting style, socio-economic status, academic resources, and a myriad of other indirect factors. In addition to the general parenting styles, there are also other behavioral factors that parents employ that also impacts their children's future.

That said, consider the following general assumptions regarding child rearing. According to leading psychologists, there are four (4) types of parenting styles.

Authoritarian Parenting: This style establishes strict rules. Failure to follow these rules results in harsh punishment. I refer to this style as the "Because I said so" style because the high demanding parent enforces strict rules without explaining the reason or rationale for the rule(s). These parents give orders; and their children must blindly obey their orders without question. Understandably, their children will usually be task-oriented, obedient individuals; but their self-esteem is typically compromised.

Authoritative Parenting: Do not get this confused with the above "Authoritarian" parenting style. This parenting style establishes structure and parameters for children's behavior, but the approach is democratic. These parents set clear and definitive boundaries, standards, and expectations but are also willing to listen to their children's questions and concerns. As you would expect, children raised by an authoritative parent are generally happy, capable, and successful in life.

Permissive Parenting: Parents who follow this parenting style set very low expectations and boundaries for their children. These parents indulge their children, are not demanding, and are extremely lenient. This is the parenting style you hear referenced when a parent says, *"I'm more their best friend than their parent."* This parent does not want the child to be angry, so the child tends to run the household.

Uninvolved or Negligent Parenting: This parent is exactly as the name implies: uninvolved. While the parent may attend to the most basic of the child's needs (shelter, food, clothing), this parent is detached from the emotional and psychological needs of the child. Obviously, these children are more likely to have issues with self-esteem, self-control, and general competency.

Of all four parenting styles, the permissive parenting style is the most concerning to me as it relates to the academic success of our children. The uninvolved/negligent parent will not be reading this book. However, the permissive parent may very well be reading it. This parent is oftentimes a loving parent who feels confused and conflicted about exerting authority over the children. The permissive parent wants the children to be happy, so the parent feels the best way to ensure their happiness is to indulge them in everything. You will overhear these parents telling others they want to be their child's "best friend."

Studies show the permissive style often leads to children who are unhappy, have issues with self-regulation and authority, and tend to perform very poorly in school.

From my own observations, children really do thrive in a very structured environment. In fact, they crave this structure. As they are forming their identity, they are relying on a structured foundation that is dependable and caring. However, an overly structured and demanding foundation can lead to the Authoritarian Parenting style.

You need to establish control and consistently maintain your authoritative presence. Our children can rely and depend on our dominant presence and have faith in our direction. Your position must be unwavering. If you demonstrate ambivalence or indifference, your child will sense it.

As parents, Arturo and I used Authoritative Parenting with our three children. We refer to our style as being "large and in charge." We are strict parents. Our children will tell you this and so will our neighbors, co-workers, and friends. However, when you ask our children how they will raise their *own* children, they will all say they will be "large-and-in-charge," strict, authoritative parents. They know it works. They have seen the results and are living them now.

Our children respect us and understand their boundaries, yet they are not fearful of us. They know they have free will, but they also realized and respected our vision for the direction of their lives.

We are strict with our words and our expectations, but we never used any form of physical or verbal punishment with our children. In fact, my children will tell you the absolute worst punishment they could possibly receive was one of my "looks." Just one look from me and they knew immediately they had misbehaved.

As "large-and-in-charge" parents, our children followed our lead in every aspect of their lives, including academics, health, social, and personal choices. You might wonder how children can be so obedient, respectful, and loving. It is the combination of authoritative parenting style coupled with the 10 Quetzal Mama Principles. When you are "large and in charge," have high expectations, and encourage your child to live up to his/her potential, you create extraordinary children.

Being "large and in charge" means setting limits, regulating behaviors, and establishing priorities.

Setting limits may refer to limiting the time your children are allowed to watch television or play video games. In the Ocampo household, television viewing is mostly limited to the weekend. Video game playing is limited to one hour per day and only during the weekend. Furthermore, television and video game playing privileges are only allowed when academic obligations (homework, projects, supplemental reading, and timed exercises) and assigned chores are completed.

Setting limits may also refer to the time your child is allowed to text or gain access to the Internet. In our household, Internet usage was exclusively limited to research for homework assignments. While we allowed our children to talk with friends on their phones, we applied the same rules regarding fulfilling their academic obligations and household chores.

Regulating behaviors is an integral part of being a "large-and-in-charge" parent. From the time our children were old enough to speak, we established firm guidelines regarding acceptable behaviors. For example, our children are not allowed to "talk back" or use disrespectful language or behavior. This includes rolling the eyes, mumbling comments of disapproval, or disobeying our instructions. There is a difference between a child challenging or questioning a particular rule or concept versus outright disobedience. While we encourage our children to use critical thinking skills and to question authority when something seems irrational or immoral, we disallow outright defiance to us (the parents).

The "large-and-in-charge" parent establishes and enforces priorities. In our household, priorities include family, spirituality, education, and service to others. To emphasize the importance of education, homework always comes first in our household. As soon as our children come home from school they immediately attend to their homework.

Another aspect of being "large and in charge" is taking your role of being the overseer of your family seriously. In this respect, I call myself "Quetzal Mama" for a reason. When anyone has insulted my children, short-changed them in an academic setting, or robbed them of anything that directly or indirectly affected their well being, clear the path! Here comes the Quetzal Mama, swooping down to protect her *Quetzalitos!*

Many Latino parents are challenged with being assertive in academic settings. I have seen parents accept school decisions that negatively impact their child's future because they are too timid to speak up on the child's behalf. I realize we are all different and that not everyone has the ability to confront individuals or respond effectively in awkward situations. However, there are various ways to work around this inability.

For example, if you feel you are too timid to approach a teacher, administrator, or other adult, why not take an advocate with you? This advocate can be your neighbor, relative, or a friend. You need to have someone with you who can advocate on your child's behalf.

If language is an issue, find a translator to assist you in these situations. Many public educational institutions, under certain circumstances, are required to provide a Spanish language translator upon request. Ask your school district about its policy on providing free Spanish language translators.

If a direct, one-on-one encounter is not your cup of tea, why not sit down and compose a letter articulating your thoughts and expectations?

A simple letter is often a very effective mode of communicating your key points and is also a useful way to document a particular situation.

Here is an example of how I dealt with a difficult campus safety issue through the use of written documentation. When my son Emilio was in the first grade, another student was bullying him. Apparently, Emilio wanted to "show me" versus "tell me" what was occurring at school. One morning, Emilio asked me to walk him to the blacktop. He had never asked me to do this, so I was intrigued. He did not want me to walk with him—only to stop at the edge of the campus and watch him. Little did I know he wanted me to be aware of a situation on his campus. I can still recall this painful moment in slow-motion, as I squatted in the corner near the cafeteria. I saw Emilio walking to put his backpack in the stack with the others. All of a sudden a student grabbed his backpack and pulled Emilio across the blacktop.

Instead of becoming hysterical, I walked briskly (but calmly) to the blacktop and separated my son from the bully. I asked Emilio for the name of the boy who attacked him. I reassured Emilio, and let him know I would handle the situation. After ensuring he was safe, I drove to work. The first thing I did was contact the Director of Student Services. I met with him in person and requested a copy of the district's anti-bullying and anti-violence policies. When I found the information I needed, I composed an email to the Principal of my son's school and copied the Director of Students Services (and his teacher). In the email, I included a copy of the district's policy and stated my expectations as to how my son's situation would be handled. I expected the district would enforce their "Zero Tolerance" policy regarding violence on campus. The next day I learned the student who harmed my son was suspended from school.

This is how we do it, parents. We don't wait for administrators or teachers to rectify the situation in our child's best interest. **We cannot**

assume someone else will be an advocate for our children. We have to be "large and in charge." Get your game on, and handle the situation for your children. Put your complaint in writing, and succinctly state your expectations. Give deadlines. This is how you get the results you need – the results that will benefit your child. *¡Sí se puede, Quetzal Mamas!*

CHAPTER 4

THOSE PESKY MYTHS

Let's cut through some bogus myths that will sabotage your implementation of the 10 Quetzal Mama Principles or deter you from helping your child reach his/her full potential.

These myths will deny your child the opportunity to realize full potential, will keep your child and future generations from fulfilling their destiny, and may prohibit your child from making a valuable contribution to humanity.

Our society desperately needs the unique contributions of Latino children. Our voice, creativity, and intellect are greatly needed. Think of previous Latino children who came to contribute in profound and inspiring ways, such as César Chávez, Astronaut José Hernandez, Carlos Santana, Dr. Quiñones-Hinojosa, Author Sandra Cisneros, or Supreme Court Justice Sonia Sotomayor. Imagine what our society would be like without their contributions? Imagine the potential your child has and how you can change the outcome of their future. Your child can contribute in a profound way with your support and belief.

Consider the following myths and ask yourself, "How many times have I bought into this negative thinking?" How often have you allowed these myths to rule your judgment?

Myth #1: My child has to be a genius to be admitted to a prestigious university or to make a profound contribution in our society.

The truth: Each year Ivy League campuses receive upwards of 35,000 applications from high school seniors. A significant percentage of denied applicants represent Valedictorians and those with perfect scores on their SATs. Conversely, a tier of students are admitted with lower SAT scores and lower GPAs. If "genius" is defined purely by academic achievement and standardized test scores, then this myth was just blown out of the water.

The truth is there are *other* characteristics your child possesses that determine his/her greatness and future potential.

Myth #2: I need to be "rich" to afford the extra activities and resources that will help my child make a profound contribution. If I am not rich, my child will not be prepared to compete.

If you read the previous chapter, "The 10 Quetzal Mama Principles," you will know *none* of the principles require a financial investment. Implementing the 10 Quetzal Mama Principles is absolutely free and only requires an investment in time and energy. My husband and I followed these ten principles exclusively to shape and to guide our children's developmental years. We are certainly not rich, nor did we hire a team of "experts," or send them to exclusive boarding schools.

Consider another example that debunks the myth about being rich: César E. Chávez. We cannot put a price tag on the profound contributions that significantly impacted the lives of farm workers and our world, yet we know he did not come from a privileged background.

Myth #3: Most children are just average. Statistically, those who contribute in a significant way to humanity are only a rare, chosen few.

Wrong. Most Latino children have incredible gifts and talents that are untapped. They were brainwashed to believe they are average, or more often, inferior. It is your role as the parent to identify the wonderful skills, talents, and ways your Latino child can contribute to our world.

Myth #4: My child will never buy this nonsense. How can I possibly convince my child s/he is destined for greatness?

To debunk this myth, I challenge you to do your own study. Visit a classroom for any grade in your district. Watch how the teacher interacts with the students. There will inevitably be the chosen "super stars" and "over achievers" in this class, and there will also be the often overlooked middle-of-the road and so-called "underachievers." What drives the superstars in the classroom? Why do they proudly raise their hands while their peers sit back and watch? You will notice quickly that a select child or group of students consistently receive positive reinforcement while the other students are either ignored or treated indifferently. They know others have high expectations of them, and they perform to the level of expectation.

The same rule is applied in your household. If you express in verbal and non-verbal ways that your child is a superstar, your child will begin acting like a superstar. I am not talking about spoiling or creating a prima donna. I am talking about instilling pride in your child by giving positive reinforcement and convincing your child that s/he is destined for greatness.

Historically, our Latino children have been cast into a role that portrays them as unsuccessful, non-competitive underachievers. When your Latino child enters the classroom, s/he may be viewed and perceived through this deficit lens. The expectation your child's teacher has may be quite different for your Latino child than his/her East Indian, Asian, or white counterparts.

Your child is destined for greatness. If you believe this, simply behave in ways to support your belief. Your child will live up to your expectation and become the leader s/he was intended to be.

PART TWO

QUETZAL MAMA K-12 STRATEGIES

IN THIS SECTION you will learn how to successfully navigate the entire K-12 system – including elementary, middle school, and high school.

CHAPTER 5

WORK THE SYSTEM

"WORK THE SYSTEM" refers to insider tools and strategies to help Latino parents navigate successfully throughout K-5, middle, and high school. As a parent, understanding the dynamics of your child's academic institution, knowing what programs and services are offered, preparing your child for each school year, and exercising parental and student rights is critical. Let's look at five strategies that will help you "work the system."

- Know Your Rights
- Know your Student's Academic Profile
- Identify Specialized Programs

- Consider an Accelerated Schedule
- Get Involved (on campus and in your child's classroom)

Know Your Rights. As Latino parents, it can be confusing, frustrating, and sometimes intimidating to contact your child's school when an issue or problem arises. For example, what do you do if any of the following occur?

- You are asked to attend a conference or meeting about your student, but the district does not provide a Spanish translator?
- A teacher insults or says something derogatory to your child;
- You wish to file a complaint against your child's teacher, counselor, or principal;
- You wish to challenge a grade issued on your student's report card;
- A teacher or administrator recommends retaining your student;
- Your child is inappropriately assigned to a program such as ELD (English Language Development), or has not advanced to mainstream English Language Arts (ELA) in an appropriate period of time;
- Your child is overlooked, bypassed, or not recommended for specialized programs or courses, although s/he has met eligibility requirements;
- Your child is being tracked into programs inconsistent with his/her intellectual abilities;
- Your student's counselor is not providing appropriate assistance.
- Your child is being bullied;
- Your child is falsely identified as being a gang member; or threatened with suspension or expulsion;
- Your child is threatened with having a permanent notation in their official academic transcript concerning academic misconduct or behavioral misconduct.

Most of us do not know our parental rights, the proper protocol, nor when to escalate a situation. While different school districts may have different board policies and procedures, there are basic rules that govern most public schools.

These basic "laws" come from the state Department of Education. A state level education law will *always* trump a school-site specific policy or rule. When investigating any of the above bulleted topics, always start with the state education code. Education code for your respective state can be found online, available to the public. Now, let's review site level policies, specific to your school site and school district.

<u>Board Policies and/or Administrative Regulations</u> What is the difference between board policies and administrative regulations? Board policies are adopted by your local Board of Trustees and they are intended to be broad in nature. Administrative regulations provide the details for each policy – the who, where, when, and how. Board Policies and Administrative Regulations should be available on your district's website. If not, call the superintendent's office to ask where you can obtain them. These are public documents. You are entitled to these documents, and the administration must comply with your request.

<u>Student and/or Parent Handbook</u> If your child did not receive a student handbook at the beginning of the school year, contact the site principal. Student handbooks contain policies, programs, calendars, and events specific to your school site.

<u>Know Your District's Chain of Command</u> Often, there are protocols established at the school site and district level that require a specific "chain of command." Knowing the hierarchy for public school districts will help you work through the system, without wasting time and energy.

State Department of Education
↑
County Office of Education
↑
Board of Trustees
↑
Superintendent
↑
Site Principal
↑
Teacher
↑
Student

The arrows above represent the hierarchal order of who reports to whom. For example, your student reports to his teacher, but his teacher reports to the site principal, and so on. If your student encounters a problem that requires your mediation, follow through this chain of command to have your problem resolved.

The Freedom of Information Act (FOIA)   FOIA is a federal law that allows you to request and to obtain certain documents from a preschool, public or private, elementary, or secondary school.

If you have asked your site administration (office staff or site principal) for a specific document and they have refused, go to the superintendent. If the superintendent refuses, go to the board of directors/ trustees. The best approach is to write a formal and concise letter, addressed to each person or persons, and ensure you have documented the delivery method (for example, "Certified Mail" or "Delivery Confirmation Receipt"). When Latino parents take these steps and adhere to this formal, methodological approach, they are most successful.

To demonstrate how Latino parents can utilize state laws, the following is an example for Spanish speaking parents requiring translation services. This language is found in California Education Code and mandates Spanish language translation of documents. Note that each state may have different provisions for translation services:

48985. (a) If 15 percent or more of the pupils enrolled in a public school that provides instruction in kindergarten or any of grades 1 to 12, inclusive, speak a single primary language other than English, as determined from the census data submitted to the department pursuant to Section 52164 in the preceding year, all notices, reports, statements, or records sent to the parent or guardian of any such pupil by the school or school district shall, in addition to being written in English, be written in the primary language, and may be responded to either in English or the primary language.

If your child attends a private school, you may not have the same rights. Private schools are not always required to adhere to the same federal and state laws as public schools. However, you should still prepare yourself with as much information as possible. For example, request the school policies, handbook, or bylaws.

A Tip for Parents! Yes, there are many regulations and policies in place for public school districts. However, don't overlook the option to challenge a rule, policy, or decision. The truth is, *there are always exceptions.* For example, if your child's counselor is not adequately serving your student or attending to their best interests, you have the right to request an alternate counselor. Or, if your student was not nominated for a particular class you have the right to challenge the decision. I've gone through this process with my own kids – from challenging teachers when they did not recommend my children for particular classes, to challenging GATE Administrators when they failed to identify my children's giftedness.

Know Your Student's Academic Profile. Your child's academic "profile" is not something that exists – it is something you will create. The profile consists of a few basic components. First, you'll want to get your hands on any standardized benchmarks, assessments, or examinations administered on behalf of your student(s). Previously, states relied on their own state-level assessment – such as the Standardized Testing and Reporting (STAR) program administered in California. However, beginning in the 2015/2016 school year, districts across the US will be utilizing the Smarter Balanced assessment system as a result of the Common Core State Standards.

Second, you'll review your student's most recent report card(s). These two items will help you better understand your child's academic abilities as well as areas for potential improvement. Finally, if your student was tested and assessed for the Gifted and Talented Education (GATE), you will want to review the results for any exams administered. These tests may include the *Otis-Lennon School Ability Test* (OLSAT) or the *Naglieri Nonverbal Ability Test* (NNAT). See "Identify Specialized Programs" below.

How is knowing your child's academic profile useful? First, it helps parents understand whether they should identify optional resources to help their student improve or master specific curriculum (math or English), such as tutoring. It also helps parents determine whether their child should pursue an accelerated schedule (see section below). The profile is also useful for parents to identify "red flags."

For example, if Esmeralda is ranked in the 99th percentile in mathematics on an annual assessment but received an inconsistent math grade or in-class assessment by her teacher, then this inconsistency should be investigated. Conversely, if Esmeralda scored in the 50th or 75th percentile in math, this will be the area you will expect the teacher to address in order for her score to be raised. Finally, this profile is useful in identifying whether your student may be a potential candidate for specialized programs such as GATE.

To recap, developing your child's academic profile will help:

- Establish a benchmark to better understand and gauge your student's academic progress;
- Understand whether your child needs additional resources, such as tutoring;
- Identify whether or not to pursue an accelerated schedule;
- Identify "red flags" such as inconsistencies between course grades and assessment tests;
- Identify whether your student may be a candidate for specialized programs, such as GATE.

Identify Specialized Programs. There are several specialized programs available for students in public school districts. To determine which resources are available in your district, county, region, or state visit your school-site or district website, County Office of Education website, State Department of Education website, or programs listed in your School Handbook. If you feel your child requires support in these areas, make sure to refer to the two sections above regarding parental/student rights and your student's academic profile.

Many state-funded programs covering language, speech, and learning disabilities will be identified early by teachers, therapists, and/or counselors in Pre-K, Kinder, and K-5. As a parent, you should know whether your child qualifies for these programs, how your child is assessed, and how the program will help your child along his/her academic pathway.

An example of a specialized program is the gifted and talented education program. Different states refer to their gifted programs with different names. In California, it is referred to as the GATE Program—which stands for Gifted and Talented Education. These gifted programs serve high-achieving students in elementary and secondary schools. If you believe your child demonstrates characteristics of a gifted student, ask for information from your district. Speak with your child's teacher to request a nomination form. Different states have different qualifying criteria, so it is important that you carefully read the guidelines for your state and county. Chapter 7, "Ignacia la Ingeniosa" also addresses gifted educational programs.

In addition to specialized programs run at the school site, district, or county level, there are also national programs for students at the elementary through postsecondary level. For example, there are several college-readiness programs including Advancement Via Individual Determination (AVID), Gear-Up, and Upward Bound, to name a few. To find a college readiness program in your state, visit the website "collegeaccess.org" and click the link to view the Program Directory.

Consider an Accelerated Schedule. An accelerated schedule is an academic plan that allows your student to advance through K-5, middle, or high school at a faster rate than his/her peers who follow a traditional schedule. This strategy is not for all students. Your child should pursue an accelerated schedule if s/he is intellectually advanced for his/her age, works well independently, and is self-motivated. Some parents might recognize this concept as "skipping a grade." While it can apply to skipping a grade level, more often it refers to bypassing certain curricula (like basic math) to advance to a higher level of math (e.g., algebra) in a shorter period of time.

Latino parents are often uninformed regarding an accelerated schedule, the process of challenging and bypassing curricula, or skipping a grade level. However, it is a parent's fundamental right to place his/ her child in a plan of study appropriate for the child's learning abilities. Since each district will have its own policy and practice regarding challenging curricula and bypassing grade levels, ask for the administrative regulations or board policies to become informed.

Another strategy is to enroll your students in courses during the summer to advance skills or to learn strategies. For example, during two consecutive summers (6th grade and 7th grade), we enrolled our children in the José Valdes Summer Math Institute. This intensive math program provided them with fundamental tools to master several mathematical concepts and strategies to accelerate their learning and succeed in tough high school math curriculum such as AP Calculus. Another acceleration option is to enroll your high school students in introductory college-level courses offered at a local community college.

With budget cuts, many public school districts only offer remedial courses during the summer. If this is the case in your district, check with other local districts and try to enroll your child in their summer courses. Keep in mind that there are many courses not typically taught during the summer (e.g., foreign language). If your child's desired course is not available in your local school district(s), consider a local community college. If neither of these options is available, consider an online course from an accredited university.

A word of caution. If your child pursues any of the above options and wishes to have the courses noted on their high school transcript, make sure you obtain a signed document *in advance* from your school's registrar. This document should confirm five items: (1) The school is granting unconditional permission for your child to obtain instruction outside of their district; (2) the school is giving standard academic credit or units for the course(s) taken; (3) the course(s) will be counted toward graduation requirements and fulfills a particular requirement;

(4) the course(s) will be documented within your student's official transcript; and (5) the course will be articulated at the potential college(s) your student will apply.

If your student is trying to bypass curricula by taking a course outside of his/her high school, you will want to get something in writing. The document must quantify the semester equivalency (e.g., equivalent to one or two semesters) and specify the category(ies) the course fulfills. For example: *Julio Garcia completed Foreign Language 2B (Course #XLT22435, Advanced Spanish) in the summer of 2015, at Latino Community College, and received an A grade. This course meets the equivalency of two semesters of Spanish 4. Therefore, Julio has met the fourth-year foreign language requirement, will receive appropriate credit (units), and will have these credits appear on his official academic transcript.*

A verbal statement by someone in the counseling staff will not be enforceable; therefore, obtain a signed document containing these items before you waste your time and money.

A powerful tip! Did you know one of the first questions asked on college applications is whether or not the student has enrolled in coursework *outside* of their high school's college-prep curriculum? The majority of students will not have taken such courses. To learn how to use this strategy to increase your child's college admission odds, bring Quetzal Mama to your high school site. See www.quetzalmama.com to learn how to host a Quetzal Mama workshop.

Keep in mind, regardless of whether your student accelerates his/her schedule by challenging the curricula, or by taking a course at another institution, districts may have a unit requirement for graduation. In other words, your student may still be required to complete a total number of units at the high school campus in order to graduate. Always check in advance with your registrar, get everything in writing, and keep copies of all submitted documents.

Get Involved (on campus and in your child's classroom). There are many ways to be involved and active in your child's academic journey from K-5 through high school. Depending on your work schedule and other factors, there are numerous ways to be involved without actually stepping foot in your child's classroom.

<u>Volunteer in your child's classroom.</u> Volunteering in your child's classroom does not have to be a formal commitment. For those of us Latino parents who work full time or have child care challenges, there are other ways we can volunteer. Volunteerism can be in the form of making copies at home, constructing projects at home, or simply donating some items to the classroom. Again, it is not the item or project that is necessarily important but the fact you are involved. When the teacher is convinced you have a vested interest in your child's academic success, so too will the teacher.

<u>Get involved on campus.</u> Get to know everything about your child's school. Join the school's parent group, view the school's website, visit the teacher's webpage, attend every school event, and get a copy of the school handbook. School events may include "Back to School Night," parent/teacher conferences, the district music festival, art exhibit, annual spelling bee, science fair, Academic Decathlon, Science Olympiad, and many other activities. Getting involved on-campus does more than just announce your physical presence. You will network with other parents, learn about opportunities for your child that may not be advertised elsewhere, and demonstrate to your child that education is a critical priority. Take your children with you to these events, and build it into your annual event schedule. Your family's attendance automatically creates a sense of community with the school.

Create a personal *connection* with your child's teacher(s). I am not talking about developing a friendship or personal relationship. I am talking about ensuring your child's elementary school teacher(s) knows who you are and acknowledges you have very high expectations for your child. Often, parents do not meet their child's teacher until "Back to School" night or parent/teacher conferences. Taking time early in the school year to establish a formal introduction will demonstrate that you are interested and invested in your child's education and that you will be watching closely.

The first step is to schedule a mini-conference with your student's teacher. This mini-conference will be scheduled at the teacher's convenience and may be only 15 to 20 minutes. Your goal at this conference is to cover two topics. First, after introducing yourself, briefly summarize your understanding of your child's academic profile (see above section). Then, succinctly state the expectations you have for your child's academic growth. For example, you may wish to highlight the need for mastery in mathematics. Second, ask the teacher what *you and your student* can do to help accomplish his/her academic goals.

You might ask the teacher where you can find additional resources for your student to supplement his/her work at home. The teacher will likely know many local programs or online tools that have helped other students through the years. See also *Chapter 8, "Set Up a Game Plan"* regarding supplemental work.

Monitor Your Child's Progress Online. Most school districts now offer parents a way to monitor their child's academic progress through the Internet. With a User ID and password, parents can review their child's pending and completed assignments, projects, and course grades. This is especially helpful for parents because we can view information real-time versus waiting for the end of the quarter, trimester, or semester report card. Monitoring your child's progress online is another way to be involved and proactive in your child's academic journey.

Let us review why it is important to "Work the System." Our Latino children too often fall through the cracks when left unguided during their academic career. Remember, your child will be in school thirteen years, plus a year of Transitional Kindergarten. That is a total of fourteen years *before* they get to college. If you are working the system and have a plan in place for your child, those fourteen years will be purposeful, positive, and productive. If, however, you allow your child's school (the teachers, principal, etc.) full responsibility for ensuring the success of your child's academic career, you may be disappointed.

To recap, "Work the System" by following these strategic actions.

- Know Your Rights—Be aware of your parental rights, administrative regulations, board policies, and state and federal laws to protect students and parents.
- Know Your Student's Academic Profile – By having this knowledge in hand, you can better maneuver through the academic pipeline as an informed parent.
- Identify Specialized Programs—Know what programs exist and take advantage by participating.
- Consider an Accelerated Schedule—Skip a grade or challenge coursework to bypass curricula.
- Get Involved—Attend campus events, schedule meetings with your child's teacher, volunteer in class or remotely, and monitor your child's academic progress online.

The most important thing you are doing through these exercises is demonstrating to your child that (1) education is the primary goal and concern of your family; (2) you and your family are invested in your child's success; and (3) you care deeply about your child's academic future. Remember, you do not have to attempt these strategies alone! Develop a team approach by asking your spouse, friend, co-worker, or other supportive individual to accompany you to these activities or to help you devise a plan.

Now that you know how to work the system, the following two chapters will help you devise an actual step-by-step academic strategy for your child.

CHAPTER 6

THINK *BACKWARDS*

BEFORE YOU READ the chapter, "Set Up a Game Plan," it is important to understand the concept of backward design. This frame of mind is the foundation to strategize your child's pathway to college. Contrary to our natural inclination of creating a forward-thinking strategy, to get your child on the fast track to college, you must think *backwards*.

What Is Thinking Backwards? "*Thinking Backwards*" is both a mental process as well as a logistical strategy. It is the act of envisioning your child's academic future, understanding where you are now with respect to achieving the desired academic goal, and taking active, deliberate, and strategic steps to successfully reach that goal.

For college aspiration, it means looking into the future – whether that's five, ten, or fifteen years from now and working backwards from the future to the present. It's the same strategy whether your student seeks to earn a BA degree at a public or private college, an AA degree at a community college, or a degree from a vocational school.

What if your child doesn't know where s/he wants to be in ten years or what college to attend? That's OK! Most students don't know that far in advance, but parents do know they want their child on track to get into the best college possible. Whichever path your student takes, you can follow the concept of "thinking backwards" to get there.

To understand the "*Thinking Backwards*" strategy, let's imagine a trip you are planning to the grocery store for a week's worth of groceries. You wouldn't drive to Latino-Mart, walk in the store, and try to devise your meals and shopping list on the spot, right? Prior to arriving at Latino-Mart, you would have considered your goal (meals for the week) and then worked backwards to plan your shopping list. You would have researched ads for the lowest prices possible and figured out a plan to make the most of your shopping dollar. You would think backwards by looking at recipes, reviewing your budget, and considering your travel time. Apply this same concept toward planning your child's education.

Let's use the concept of *thinking backwards* for a student we will call "Javier." Javier's academic goal is to be admitted to the prestigious Engineering and Applied Sciences program at Harvard University. Now, this is a fictitious scenario, intended to help us work through each step of a backward design process. Certainly, there are no guaranteed steps to ensure admission to Harvard. However, for the students I've coached through the years who received admission to Harvard, their profiles are very similar to the profile I will share below. These students were not "lucky" nor was there some mysterious force that compelled an admissions officer to admit them! They strategically mapped out their pathway beginning in middle school.

STEP ONE - *THINK BACKWARDS* FROM COLLEGE ADMISSION OFFER TO HIGH SCHOOL

The first step backward from an admission offer from Harvard would be to envision how four years of high school resulted in the desired outcome. In taking this first step we must realistically acknowledge that things won't miraculously fall together into place. Each year must be planned methodically, leading toward our desired goal.

Thinking Backwards, Javier and his parents reviewed the profile of admitted students to Harvard's engineering program. They discovered a pattern of three standardized exams that most admitted students took and scored relatively high.

They discovered the majority of admitted engineering students had scored 5's on AP Chemistry, AP Physics, and AP Calculus exams. As well, these students scored between 700 and 800 on the SAT Math portion or 91-99 on the ACT Math portion. They also scored in the 700 to 800 range on the Math Level II SAT Subject Test.

Armed with statistical data, Javier's parents realized their son would need to carefully plan these exams. In addition to *backward* designing exam dates, they would also need to *backward* design a test preparation program.

Remember, these scores referenced are for one of the most competitive universities in the world. Your child certainly does not need a perfect 5 on every AP exam, nor an 800 score in math in order to be admitted to a solid university! To identify the admitted student profile at the top three campuses your student wishes to pursue, visit each campus' undergraduate admissions website. Note the SAT scoring rubric changed in 2016 with a new maximum score of 1600. To learn more about these terms and concepts, see the Glossary.

Step Two – *Think Backwards* from High School to Middle School

Before Javier even stepped foot on his high school campus as a freshman, he and his parents utilized the *Thinking Backwards* strategy beginning in middle school. While Javier was in 6th grade, he and his parents identified the *right* high school for Javier to attend by following the following four strategies:

#1: Find the *Right* High School Campus. When considering a high school campus, first identify any specialized programs, resources, or academies your student wishes to participate. These programs may include a STEM-related or technology academy, an Honors Program, a Visual & Performing Arts academy, or Leadership program to name a few. Map out the eligibility requirements, deadlines for applications (if any), and orientation dates to become familiar with the programs. These specialized programs may require nominations or recommendations from middle school staff, so prepare in advance for this process.

Some Districts offer inter-district transfer to particular magnet schools or high performing high schools. Some counties offer intra-district transfers for such schools. Additionally, some charter school campuses enroll students via a lottery system. Javier decided to pursue enrollment at his District's high school Space & Engineering Academy.

Having researched the Space & Engineering Academy, Javier and his parents learned this specialized academy required many items in order for application eligibility. Some of the required items included a letter of recommendation from a middle school teacher or counselor, a math and science assessment exam, and completion of specific math and science class(s) with a grade B or above. This knowledge was extremely helpful for Javier and his parents to work *backwards* in order for Javier to be a competitive candidate for admission to the academy.

#2: Be Prepared to Succeed! Now that the high school type has been identified, Javier should enroll in a campus with a strong record of graduation and college readiness. Consider these key factors:

- What percentage of students graduate *and* complete subject requirements for college eligibility?
- What percentage of students meet or exceed proficiency standards in core subjects?
- How many college-prep courses are available – such as "Advanced Placement" or "International Baccalaureate" for students?

#3: Map Out the Curriculum. Once the high school was identified and selected, Javier and his parents examined the course offerings in order to map out the curriculum. They obtained the high school course catalog from the school's website under "Counselling Department." If your high school's catalog is not online, call the school to find out where to obtain a copy. Once Javier identified the courses he wished to enroll, he and his parents mapped out the order in which he would enroll in specific courses. Beginning with his first year (9th grade, aka "freshman") curriculum they determined which prerequisites (if any) were required for enrollment so that they could attend to these requirements while Javier was still in middle school.

#4: Get College Savvy! Just because Javier found an ideal school and mapped out curriculum for four years of high school, does not mean he will be college savvy! It is important for students to become educated about the college admission process in order to understand deadlines, application components, and financial aid. Identify college-readiness programs available at the school site, district, or country including Advancement Via Individual Determination (AVID), Gear-Up, and Upward Bound, to name a few. To find a college readiness program in your state, visit the website collegeaccess.org and view the program directory.

Step Three – *Think Backwards* from Middle School to Elementary (K-5)

In middle school, Javier knew he needed to be in advanced math and science classes to be accepted into the high school Space and Engineering Academy. Therefore, he planned his curriculum and extracurricular activities with this goal in mind. He was in Advanced Science, participated in Science Olympiad, and was a member of the chess team.

Step back again and contemplate how Javier was selected for Advanced Science when he arrived in middle school. Javier knew he would need to obtain a letter of recommendation as a requirement for Advanced Science before the end of sixth grade. There is only one Advanced Science class with 30 students in Javier's entire middle school of 1,500 students.

How did he get selected? How did he know this program existed? Javier's parents worked backwards from middle school to elementary school. While Javier was in elementary school, his parents visited the middle school, talked with counselors, visited the school website, and joined a parent group. Once they discovered this program, they were determined to find out how Javier could be admitted.

The Advanced Science program in middle school required an entrance essay, a minimum GPA, and a recommendation from his sixth grade science or math teacher. Having worked backward from these requirements, Javier and his parents approached each requirement with a specific strategy.

For the teacher recommendation, Javier's parents helped him establish a personal relationship with his sixth-grade science teacher, with the goal of obtaining a letter of recommendation at the end of his sixth-grade year. His parents guided Javier to conduct extra credit assignments, to meet with his teacher after class to discuss topics of interest, and to check out library books of scientific research and share his findings with his teacher.

If you feel these behaviors are self-serving or disingenuous, remind yourself of your child's higher purpose. If your child truly desires to be part of a program like Advanced Science, then you must do everything in your means to increase your child's chances. This program is a unique and rewarding exploration of science where your child will work on interesting projects, attend field trips, conduct research projects, and work alongside peers who share the same interest.

Most importantly, Javier will be in a classroom with a teacher who has high expectations of every student in the class. There are 30 students who will be selected. Do not believe for a moment the other 29 successful students were just "lucky." It is more likely they had active parents who guided their child's progress. Your child deserves to be in that classroom as much as any other child. It is your job to make sure s/he gets there.

How was all of this possible for Javier? Javier walked on campus armed with a solid academic strategy because his *parents* prepared him far in advance for these opportunities. His parents gave him a roadmap. His parents worked *backwards* each step of the journey from Harvard, high school, middle school, and elementary school. His parents applied

The *10 Quetzal Mama Principles* and then followed the steps outlined in this book to ensure Javier would make it to his freshman year at Harvard.

Thinking backwards is a bit like playing chess. You need to think several steps ahead so that you can devise a "backward" plan to get you there. A helpful visual exercise in "thinking backwards" is to create a flowchart. To create your flowchart, you will gather several documents in advance. These include the following.

- The Academic Major (e.g., mechanical engineering)—This is generally found on the college's "Academic Major" webpage.
- College Preparatory Requirements—This list of required or recommended high school courses is generally found on the college admissions page.
- Course Guides—The guides from your middle school and high school can be obtained from the counseling office or school website.
- Specialized Programs for K-8 (Such as "Advanced Science", GATE, or AVID)—These are generally found on the County Office of Education website.

Important Tip! Read Chapter 8 (*"Set Up a Game Plan"*), specifically the section, *The Big Four*, to learn four components that should be included on your flowchart.

Once you obtain the above documents, you will be able to fill in the names of the specific courses (by semester and year), working backward from high school, to middle school, to elementary school. This chart will help you map out your plan and give you an easy, visual reference point.

Now that we understand the "Thinking Backwards" strategy Javier undertook, let's look at how this rolled out in four years.

SAMPLE *THINKING BACKWARDS* STRATEGY (4 YEARS OF HIGH SCHOOL)

In his senior year in high school, Javier was a member of the competitive Space and Engineering Academy, President of MEChA, a member of MESA, and a member of the Academic Decathlon and Science Olympiad teams. He completed 400 hours of community service at the Boys and Girls Club and was a member of "Xochipilli," the folklorico dance troupe.

In addition to these prestigious merits, Javier was also a semi-finalist in the Siemens Math and Science Competition and was a summer engineering intern through the Society of Hispanic Professional Engineers (SHPE) in his sophomore and junior years.

Javier knew in advance which college preparatory courses were required to fulfill college entrance requirements (refer to Chapter 8, "Set Up a Game Plan"). However, to be a competitive candidate for Harvard's engineering program, Javier needs to have completed *the most rigorous* mathematics and science curricula offered at his school. Fortunately, Javier's enrollment in the Space and Engineering Academy put him on track to complete AP Calculus by his senior year.

In addition to the academic requirements, you will also want to "*think backwards*" regarding scholarships, leadership programs, and internship programs. Visit the websites of these types of programs that are tailored to your student's interests and academic major. Read the guidelines and requirements for these programs so that you can "*think backwards*" and map out a plan to help your child become an extremely competitive candidate. When the time comes to apply, your student will be prepared to secure many internships, scholarships, and leadership programs while in high school.

Take a moment to think about what you just read. The above scenarios of "*thinking backwards*" rely on the parent being proactive and taking an advocacy role in the child's academic career. It requires the parent to believe the child has every right to be in highly selective programs and deserves every academic opportunity available.

However, in Latino culture, we are taught early in life (mostly through our strict adherence to Catholicism) that life's opportunities are "in God's hands" or as a result of "God's will." While I am certainly not diminishing the power of our religion (I am proudly Catholic), I am saying that placing our children's future into an abstract realm and wiping our hands free—rather than claiming an advocacy role and taking charge—is not helpful and is self-defeating.

Relying on the prophetic belief that our child's destiny is out of our hands is unrealistic and counterproductive. Yes, it might be more convenient and less stressful to take the easy road and rely on teachers or counselors to set the path for our students. However, I urge you to ignore our Latino cultural tendency of differing to teachers and instead follow advice found in Benjamin Franklin's Poor Richard's Almanac of 1757: "God helps them who help themselves."

CHAPTER 7

Ignacia la Ingeniosa

RECALL IN THE preface we discussed *Resilient Rodrigo*? Well, *Ignacia la Ingeniosa* is his favorite *tia*. Ignacia finds every opportunity to help her Latino children succeed. She goes above and beyond the gates of information available at her child's school or educational community. Ignacia goes rogue! She reads books, researches websites, talks with teachers and parents, and is up in everyone's business! That's our Ignacia and we love her.

Unfortunately, not everyone is born with the personality disposition of an *Ignacia la Ingeniosa*. Therefore, in this chapter I will share six different resources that give parents a significant advantage in learning how to identify tools, resources, programs, and strategies to help their children succeed in their trajectory to college.

- Internet
- Mentors
- National Organizations
- School Staff (Teachers, Counselors, Administrators or Site Principals)
- Programs—Specialized
- Books

The Internet. The Internet is Ignacia's friend. Ignacia will begin her Internet search by utilizing a strategy I share with parents called the "Funnel Approach." This approach refers to beginning the search narrowly and then expanding outward, like a funnel. In other words, we "start local" and go "national." Using the Funnel Approach, Ignacia will scour the Internet for local opportunities first. Then, after exhausting local resources, she will expand to county, regional, state, and national resources.

Locally, Ignacia will likely find resources such as free public library programs including chess clubs and reading programs, specialized classes through the local Parks & Recreation Department, and free programs offered through the local District Office of Education. Next, Ignacia will start searching for regional programs that may be of interest to her children.

Examples include a regional robotics club, a youth symphony orchestra, university extensions for middle and high school students, or empowerment programs such as Latinas in STEM, to name a few. Finally, Ignacia will begin searching for national organizations that may have local chapters. In going through the steps to identify resources for her

74

children, Ignacia will most likely learn of other programs and resources along the way.

A key strategy in maximizing the Internet as a resource is to identify programs related to your child's interests. For example, if your daughter is interested in architecture, start researching everything related to architecture. Using architecture as a keyword, begin a search string such as "architecture, high school, Latina, Texas." If you do not yield many results with this search, broaden your search using only "architecture and Latina." Always start with a narrow search and broaden to identify resources specific to your child's interests and geographical location.

When you begin collecting this information from online searches, you will find there are many programs that are suitable for your child but not presently available (because of the child's age). That's OK! Keep a running list of all of these programs, their deadlines, and the application components. These programs could be internships, workshops, mentorships, scholarships, etc. Don't worry about what to do with this information right now. Once you read the following chapter, "Set up a Game Plan," you will see how all of this fits into your overall academic strategy.

Mentors. A mentor is an accomplished individual who has "been there, done that," so to speak. It is someone who can expose your student to real-life examples, provide factual and relevant information, and give your child the basic tools they need to get started. Mentorship is a critical resource to help Latino students attain success in academic and career goals.

Mentors help our students learn what is required to reach their goal, to identify an effective path to get there, and to develop strategies for each step of the way. Most parents are not 100 percent knowledgeable about every career or every academic pursuit, which is why our Latino students need a mentor.

Mentorship does more than establish a "connection." The benefits of mentorship is well documented including establishing personal contacts to help our youth meet important industry professionals, identify internships, introduce students to professional resources and organizations, and develop important interpersonal skills for interviews and professional interaction. However, one of the most important aspects of mentorship is the positive psychological validation it will offer your student.

Mentoring programs are designed to assist students from various academic and socioeconomic backgrounds. The first step in identifying a mentor is to know where to look. There are many national organizations, state-wide agencies, and regional programs that offer free mentorship opportunities. The following is a sample of national programs that offer student mentorship. Keep in mind, these organizations serve students from elementary to high school to community college and beyond:

Organization	Website
Ace Mentor Program	acementor.org
Big Brothers/Big Sisters	bbbs.org
City Year	cityyear.org
Girls Inc.	girlsinc.org
Hispanic Alliance for Career Enhancement (HACE)	haceonline.org
Hispanic Heritage Foundation (LOFT Fellowship Program)	hispanicheritage.org
Latinas in Stem Foundation	latinasinstem.com
Student Mentor	studentmentor.org

However, the best mentor for your student may not be with a national or regional organization. The ideal mentor for your student may be right in your own community. There are many local professionals who wish to help students who are driven and industrious. I served as a mentor in the Big Brothers/Big Sisters Program and Friends Outside for several years. Both of my mentees are college graduates. My children also sought out mentors to guide them as high school students while they were making critical decisions concerning particular disciplines and colleges.

However, it seems that the powerful and positive traits of resilience and independence we learn in our Latino culture hampers our ability to reach out and ask for help. Therefore, although it may be an uncomfortable task, we do need to take the important step of asking for assistance.

National Organizations. There are several key organizations whose mission is to help Latino students. These organizations are listed on my website, and I am listing *just a few* of them here.

- Conexión Americas
- League of United Latin American Citizens (LULAC)
- Mexican American Legal Defense and Educational Fund (MALDEF)
- National Council of La Raza (NCLR)
- Parent Institute for Quality Education (PIQE)
- Society for the Advancement of Chicanos and Native Americans in Science (SACNAS)

Additionally, there are other national organizations not specific to Latinos, but very useful. The following are a few of such organizations:

Academic Decathlon	National Association of Student Councils
Future Business Leaders of America	National Speech & Debate Association
HOSA – Future Health Professionals	Rotary International
Junior Achievement	Science Olympiad
Mathematical Association of America	Technology Student Association

Membership in these organizations may give access to specialized programs and internship or scholarship opportunities. In addition, many of these organizations have formal and informal mentorship programs established. Participation in these programs helps your student develop teamwork skills, builds confidence presenting in front of large audiences, and is ideal to have listed on your student's college application.

School Staff. Teachers. A teacher can serve your student in more ways than teaching the academic curricula in the classroom. Teachers can recommend your student for specialized programs and awards; and they can provide letters of recommendation. A teacher can also serve as a role model for your child or help your child navigate through the school system. Most teachers have worked with hundreds, if not thousands, of students throughout their career and can be a great source of wisdom.

Counselors. Most students believe counselors only review graduation requirements, college preparatory requirements, or give overrides for courses. However, counselors can be a valuable resource for your student because they are often the front line when Admissions officers call or the first to know about a competitive scholarship or internship program. Counselors are typically those in the best position to recommend students for such programs.

With high counselor-to-student ratios, most counselors do not have the leisure of meeting and developing personal relationships with all students. Therefore, have your student schedule appointments with the counselor at least twice per year. When the time comes, the counselor can write a qualified letter of recommendation.

Administrators or Site Principals. Students often forget their middle and high school principal has the honor of making decisions and recommendations that impact a student's academic career. For example, a principal can generally hand pick (or approve the selection) which student(s) may give a keynote speech, which can serve on a special student board or committee, or whom to nominate for a prestigious leadership program.

It is wise for your student(s) to attempt to create a personal relationship with the site administrator. While many middle school sites have upwards of 1,500 students, and some high school campuses have as many as 3,000 students, it is important that our students make an effort to know their site administrator.

In addition, have your student meet and establish a rapport with the Superintendent. The relationship forged will serve your student in the future. The superintendent can recommend your student for prestigious positions within the district and oftentimes provides a select group of students with academic opportunities not known or available to the majority of the student body. A letter of recommendation from a superintendent will go a long way.

Programs—Specialized. There are many programs invaluable for Latino students in K-5, middle, and high school. Some of the programs are state-specific, and others are national. For example, the Gifted and Talented Education (GATE) Program is a free program for public K-12 schools in the U.S. A few national programs for high school students include the Academic Decathlon and Science Olympiad.

Each city, county, and school district will have its own academic programs for students. You will need to investigate which programs are available and funded in your district or geographical region. An easy way to find these local resources is to visit the website of your local County Office of Education. However, don't limit your child's exposure to school-site or district-wide resources. Consider taking your children to local exhibitions, conferences, or speaking engagements.

Books. Books are an easy way to learn about a topic of interest. Books can be used by your child to consider various disciplines of study, to view samples of projects or programs that others have successfully implemented (like science fair projects or historical essays), or to learn more about a particular subject.

I believe in the power of knowledge and arming ourselves with as much useful information as possible. However, finding the right books can be frustrating, time consuming, and expensive. Fortunately, there are a few things we can do to offset costs and minimize time spent searching for quality books.

First, we can visit online book clearinghouses like Amazon or Good Reads to find out which books are highly rated. It's as simple as entering the name of a particular topic and viewing results. For example, if you enter "best book for Latino college admissions" on Amazon, the "Flight of the Quetzal Mama" will appear as the number one book! Once you identify suitable books, you can order them from your local public library. Additionally, we can also take advantage of less expensive E-books and other downloadable options.

Speaking of resources, you won't want to miss out on Quetzal Mama's useful articles, website for program information, and Facebook page for timely tips and other resources:

Websitewww.quetzalmama.com
Facebook Pagefacebook.com/Quetzalmama
Blogquetzalmama.blogspot.com

CHAPTER 8

SET UP A GAME PLAN

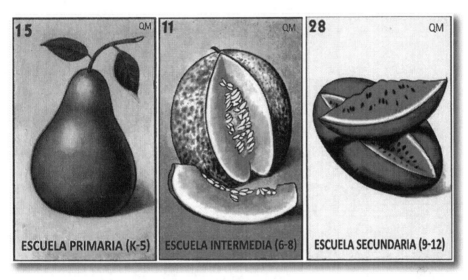

15 QM	11 QM	28 QM
ESCUELA PRIMARIA (K-5)	ESCUELA INTERMEDIA (6-8)	ESCUELA SECUNDARIA (9-12)

Now that you understand the concept of "Thinking Backwards," learned tips by "*Ignacia la Ingeniosa*" and know how to "Work the System," you're ready to set up your game plan. The components of your game plan will be determined by age and grade-level and are laid out in chronological order below.

K-5 (Grades Kinder-5)

- Know grade-level content standards.
- Supplement your child's daily work.
- Cultivate an Early Reader: *One Hour Per Day Reading Rule.*
- Enhance performance on standardized testing.

- Identify specialized programs.
- Participate in extracurricular activities.

Middle School (Grades 6-8)

- Anticipate College Preparatory Requirements.
- Know the "Big Four" requirements.
- Maintain an accelerated schedule.

High School

- Focus on GPA, class rank, and rigorous curriculum.
- Strategize college admission related examinations.
- Strategize extracurricular activities.

Kindergarten – Fifth Grade. For most parents, the K-5 years will fly by. And, for parents in California, kindergarten now starts earlier. A new law was recently enacted to create Transitional Kindergarten – a two-year kindergarten experience for students whose birthday is between September and December. This program is ideal for students who are too young to start kindergarten because of the birthday cutoff and gives these students a one-year head start.

To help parents understand what to expect and how to plan ahead for their K-5 students, I'm providing some basic pointers.

Know Grade-Level Content Standards. Knowing what your student will be learning *before* s/he starts the school year will help prepare your student for success. Knowing what *should* be learned and mastered at each grade level is equally important. I encourage you to find your state's Department of Education website and search for their content standards and state-adopted curriculum framework.

What are academic content standards? Content standards may be referred to by a different name in your state. Generally, they are K-12 academic standards that describe the content taught and learned, on a grade-by-grade basis. Content standards focus on the essential core knowledge and skills your student should be acquiring at each grade level.

For example, if your child attends public school in California, you may obtain content standards for each K-12 grade by visiting the California Department of Education website and searching for "grade level curriculum." In addition, the state-adopted curriculum framework for K-12 in California is listed on this site under "Curriculum and Instruction." Here, you will also find the Common Core State Standards adopted by the State Board of Education.

Knowing the content standards is only part of the equation. As an active parent, you can also assist your child in the learning process by supplementing daily work.

Supplement Your Child's Daily Work. Supplementing your student's workload each day is an investment. Yes, it's more work for your child(ren), but the academic benefits are numerous. I encourage parents to utilize free (online) tools to supplement their children's daily work. Some of these tools include the site www.ixl.com. This unique site provides fun and interactive exercises for Pre-K through 8th Grade. For each grade level, they list the cognitive skills required with timed activities. In addition, they have listed State Standards for fifty U.S. states.

Another effective (and free) source to supplement your child's learning is the non-profit video tutoring website www.khanacademy.org. This site is generally helpful for Grades 5 and above. As of today, Khan Academy provides more than 5,500 free tutorial videos and 100,000 practice exercises. They cover nearly every academic subject including math, science, computer programming, history, art history, economics, and more. In addition, their video content is translated into Spanish!

The first key in supplementing your child's daily work is to establish a pattern early in their academic careers. Children thrive on routines, patterns, and high expectations. By establishing a firm rule in your home – such as 20 minutes of math drills each day, your children will become accustomed to this practice and it will become part of their daily ritual. The second key is to explain to your children why they are engaging in daily routines. Be clear that you are enforcing these daily practices to help them become prepared for college.

One Hour Per Day Reading Rule – The first step in supplementing your child's daily work is to engage them in reading. Reading is so closely tied to college admissions that I created a special workshop entitled, *"The One Hour Per Day Reading Rule"* exclusively for Latino parents of K-5 students. In my workshop, I teach parents the value of instilling this practice very early as well as how to develop and cultivate an avid reader.

To start, introduce your children to reading before they begin Kindergarten by reading to them and having them read age-appropriate picture books. Remember, it's not so important what they are reading. What's important is that they are reading and learning every day. Make sure to have a series of books on hand, so that you are not scrambling to find age-appropriate reading materials.

Once your children begin first grade, you should gradually increase reading time by 10 minutes each day. Begin with 20 or 30 minutes, build to 45 minutes, and gradually move up to 60 minutes. By the time your child is in third grade, s/he should be reading at least one hour each day. Additionally, it is encouraged that you have your child read books at least one grade level above his/her current level.

Make it interesting! To ensure I had interesting books for my kids at all times, I would do a search on Amazon.com and Goodreads.com using a phrase like, "Best books for 7 year olds." I would do this each year for all my kids' grade levels. Once I identified these books, I would copy the name of the book into my Public Library search engine. Nine out of ten times, my local library stocked my desired books at one of many local branches. I would order copies to be delivered to my local branch. This way, I continually provided my kids with highly recommended books and it didn't cost me a penny!

Building this habit of reading one hour per day extends your child's vocabulary and introduces him/her to different concepts, geography, culture, and politics. The larger payoff, however, is when your child takes the SAT or ACT in high school. Studies show students who are sustained, voracious readers perform in the highest percentile in the Critical Reading and Writing portion of these exams. There you go.

Focus on Math and Reading Drills. Your student will be taking several assessments throughout the year, regardless of the grade level. To help your child earn high marks in these assessments, supplement their daily homework with a few timed activities.

To enrich your children's mastery of mathematics, try supplementing their daily homework with 20 minute timed multiplication and division exercises. There are many free templates online – just print them, grab a stopwatch and a pencil, and go! To enhance reading comprehension skills, ask your children to read a selected chapter from a book. After completing their reading assignment, ask them a series of questions to gauge their reading comprehension. It can be as simple as, "What were the names of the characters?" and "What was the main issue or problem discussed?"

Enhance Performance on Standardized Testing. Remember, your student will have learned various concepts, rubrics, formulas, and theory throughout the 10-month academic year. Unless your student is practicing these concepts consistently, s/he will likely forget the formulas, steps, and rules by the end of the school year (when mandatory state testing occurs). To help your student refresh and feel more confident, I recommend the following strategies.

First, ask your student's teacher (in early Spring) for practice tests or to provide the name of an online site where your student can conduct practice tests for mathematics, English/Language Arts, and Science. Second, visit the helpful website, www.ixl.com. This site covers content standards from Pre-Kindergarten through middle school. It is a great resource because the IXL content is aligned with each state's Common Core Standards and therefore, a wonderful way to help your children prepare for standardized exams.

Identify Specialized Programs. By the time your child starts first grade, your child's teacher will already begin identifying the top 1 – 5 percent of the students to nominate for your district's intellectually "gifted" program. If you believe your kindergartner may be a future candidate for such a program, read chapter 5, "Work the System," for more information.

In California, we refer to this program as "GATE," which stands for Gifted and Talented Education. Your state may call it something similar. For example, in Massachusetts it is called "Academically Advanced Education"; in Iowa, "Gifted & Talented"; and in Florida, "Gifted Education."

I will use GATE as an acronym in this chapter to represent any gifted and talented program in your region. A GATE program will expose your child to a more advanced and rigorous curriculum and surround him/her with other high-achieving students. However, in my opinion, the most important benefit your child will receive by participating in any gifted program is the symbolic "tap" on the shoulder. When our

Latino students' intelligence has been validated by the "gifted" label, they will absolutely perform to their designated abilities.

If your child is an English Language Learner (ELL), it is important your child's teacher not rely solely on your child's ability to express gifted qualities through English language. Unfortunately, our ELL students are challenged by overcoming the bias that limited English fluency correlates to limited academic abilities. Studies show parents are excellent identifiers of a child's giftedness. Therefore, if you believe your ELL student has high academic potential, ask that your student be evaluated with an assessment tool not limited to expression in the English language. Remember, the demonstration of creativity (in the material sense), mathematical ability, leadership, memory, or any of adopted forms of identifying "giftedness" is not required to be expressed in English!

Parents, keep in mind that our Latino children, as well as children belonging to other historically underrepresented groups, are still disproportionately under-represented in "gifted" programs. This is compounded when the assessment tools are exclusively based on the dominant cultural perspective.

When we lived in Dublin, California, our daughter Gabi was "assessed" for the GATE program. One of her tests was to gauge her leadership ability. To test Gabi's leadership ability, the test administrator gave Gabi the following scenario: She was in charge of the "janitorial help" at her school campus. Her job was to make sure the "mess" got cleaned up. Needless to say, the topic caused Gabi to feel awkward and self-conscious. Because Gabi was quite shy at that time (second grade), her strategy to get the "mess" cleaned up at her school campus was most likely very different compared to her peers (who may have been extroverted with an assertive personality disposition).

In Latino culture, we do not necessarily view positive leadership qualities as being dictatorial, loud, or demanding. In fact, I would argue the opposite—that Latinos commonly use democratic ways to achieve a community goal. I don't know whether Gabi failed this particular test, but I do know she was bewildered by the scenario. She asked me why she was told to be a "janitor." My point is that something seeming to be a predictor or confirmation of giftedness is often based on cultural "norms" and bias. Therefore, Latino parents need to be vigilant in their efforts to have their children assessed fairly and accurately.

Participate in Extracurricular Activities. Around the third grade, many students begin participating in extracurricular activities. These types of activities might include the annual spelling bee, chess club, drama club, science fair competition, etc. A more detailed explanation and strategy for "extracurricular activities" is found in Chapter 13, "Extracurricular Activities."

In addition to on-campus extracurricular activities and competitions, there are likely district or county sponsored student competitions. To determine which programs are available in your county, go to your County Office of Education website to find links to their pages. Since the programs are publicly funded, their availability will be advertised and open to all students who express interest or qualify.

These K-8 activities are typically not as competitive as the high school level. For students with specialized skills or talents, there are also *privately* funded regional and national academic competitions. For example, the DuPont Challenge is an essay competition for students from seventh grade through twelfth grade who are interested in science.

I emphasize the importance of these extracurricular activities and competitions for three reasons: (1) They will help your child explore areas outside of the classroom curriculum; (2) they will help prepare your child for higher level competitions in middle school and high school; and, most importantly (3) they will raise your child's self-confidence.

What if your child is shy, has performance anxiety, or is reluctant to perform in front of others? This happened to our son Emilio during his very first spelling bee competition. Standing in line as he waited to register and have his number pinned to his shirt, he was visibly trembling with fear. His behavior caught me and my husband off guard and we felt empathy for him as he walked up to the podium. When he spoke his first challenge word, his voice was trembling; he had tears in his eyes. We maintained a positive expression and gave him a "thumbs up," knowing we had some work to do. Instead of giving up and conceding any future activities dealing with stage presence, we brainstormed. Our solution was to find a speech and debate team and get him enrolled.

Remember that the Chapter 7, "*Ignacia la Ingeniosa*," recommends utilizing the Internet as a resource tool? That's exactly what we did. We searched for the nearest speech and debate program. Unfortunately, it was a three-hour round trip to the nearest program. However, re-read the Quetzal Mama Principle: "The Quetzal Mama Principle is the belief your child has a greater purpose in life, is obligated to fulfill that purpose, and that **you will do everything possible for your child to realize this purpose.**"

The emphasis on "You will do everything possible for your child to realize this purpose" is to remind you that "everything possible" sometimes involves a lot of work, time, resources, and sacrifices. After researching this particular speech and debate program, we realized the program had exceptional benefits for Emilio.

First, the head coach was a nationally renowned speech and debate coach. Second, we knew Emilio's involvement in this program would help him with his stage fear. Finally, Emilio would meet other talented students in the process and would learn valuable skills. After the first six months of participating in this program, Emilio overcame his stage fright. Subsequently, he conducted many on-stage presentations. Today, he is a member of his 8th grade class Speech & Debate Club and plans to compete in high school as well.

While it is not convenient or time effective for my husband and me to spend three hours driving and four hours waiting for his workshop (for a total of seven hours on Saturdays), it was a great investment for Emilio's future. If you find opportunities for your children that are out of your geographic region or a big time investment, consider the impact on your child's future. Step up Quetzal Mamas!

4th Grade – *Think Backwards.* You will read in the next section how 5th grade is a pivotal time for parents. However, before we read about the deadlines in 5th grade, we should put on our "*Thinking Backwards*" sombrero to get into the right mindset and be proactive.

In early spring of your student's 4th grade year, begin *Thinking Backwards* from middle school. In the next section you will quickly learn how many decisions you'll need to make by the spring of your son or daughter's 5th grade year. These decisions will impact your student's success in middle school and high school.

For example, knowing that your student will have many options – including public middle school programs, private or Catholic schools, charter schools, magnet schools and specialized academies, we'll need to *Think Backwards* to be prepared. The following are a few tasks to consider:

- Troubleshoot prerequisites (GPA, course requirements) for specialized programs;
- Develop relationships with teachers or site principals (Letters of Recommendation);

- Determine qualifying criteria for scholarships at a private or Catholic school;
- Identify qualifying test scores for competitive magnet campuses or academies;
- Enroll in tutoring/prep course to receive a competitive score on assessment exams.

5th Grade is a Pivotal Moment – The transition from elementary (K-5) to middle school (6-8) creeps up on us parents! All of a sudden, it's spring of your student's 5th grade year. You realize this when you get the flyer reminding you that you must enroll in middle school by a specific date. And, you must select the class schedule. You are tasked with so many decisions: Should your student enroll in the middle school zoned for your neighborhood? What about charter schools or specialized academies? Is your child a strong candidate for private or Catholic schools? What about magnet programs? What classes will your child be placed? Is s/he required to take placement exams? Is s/he on track for courses aligned with the high school college prep program?

Don't worry parents, Quetzal Mama is here to help. I want you to know if you do one thing before your child reaches the 5th grade you will be prepared. I want you to get a big red pen and circle the first day back from break in your child's second semester of 5th grade. This should be sometime in January. Why January? Because the application deadline for most programs, academies, and lotteries, occur around February or March every year.

February and March is typically the time frame when nearly all public schools request class curriculum/enrollment, verification of enrollment for designated school sites, and applications for many school programs and academies. To help you prepare for the most common deadlines, I'm providing the following tasks for you to consider:

Middle School. In no time your child will be graduating from a K-5 school and entering middle school or graduating from a K-8 school and beginning high school. This time will fly. Many students are, unfortunately, unprepared for the quick transition. Way before they complete the sixth grade, you will need to map out their high school requirements.

This is the period of time you will strategize which pathway, academy, or pre-college (AP or IB) program your student will pursue in high school. Knowing which of these programs your student will pursue will help you identify the curriculum, extracurricular activities, and competitions that will make your student a competitive college applicant.

Anticipate College Preparatory Requirements. What are college preparatory requirements? These are the courses students take in high school (with a Grade C or better) to meet the general eligibility requirements for college. Why am I talking about high school now? Remember, to be prepared we must, "*Think Backwards.*" Far in advance of transitioning to high school, your student needs to be on track when s/he enters middle school.

Determine the college preparatory requirements in your state. In California, we refer to these requirements as the "A—G" subject requirements. Most four-year state colleges and private universities have pre-determined college preparatory courses identified on their website. Once you are familiar with the requirements, determine whether there are any *pre-requisites* to these high school courses so that your student can take these in middle school.

An example of the "A—G" subject requirements for California State University and University of California are as follows. Note that each high school will have their own graduation requirements, in addition to these subject requirements. Selective colleges will typically recommend coursework that exceeds these minimum requirements.

A–G	University of California (UC) & California State College (CSU)	Required	Recommended
A	History/Social Science	2 years	
B	English	4 years	
C	Mathematics	3 years	4 years
D	Laboratory Science (Biology, Chemistry, Physics)	2 years	3 years
E	World Language	2 years	3 years
F	Visual & Performing Arts	1 year	
G	College Preparatory Electives	1 year	

I encourage students to focus on the college preparatory requirements for competitive universities, versus focusing on minimum college entrance requirements. This strategy will allow your student greater opportunities and options when it comes time to apply to college. However, if your child's abilities and interests are not consistent with a competitive university, focus on the minimum requirements.

Important Note! Did you know that in California, currently only 20% of Latino public high school graduates are meeting the A-G requirements? Stated another way, that means that 80% of our students are NOT eligible to enter a University of California or California State University campus. Stated yet another way, that means that 65% of California Latino high school graduates are enrolling in community colleges and NOT 4-year universities. Better start *Thinking Backwards* to ensure your student is on track to graduate *and* meet the college eligibility requirements!

Know the "Big Four" Requirements. The following are four simultaneous strategies designed by Quetzal Mama to help your student maximize options for college admission:

QUETZAL MAMA'S BIG FOUR
(Four Simultaneous Strategies)

Graduation Requirements
College Preparatory Requirements
Private or Competitive College Requirements
Discipline-Specific (College Major) Requirements

Consider the challenge of accomplishing the above four strategies simultaneously, and it is no wonder students have a difficult time. Students must know simultaneously what is required to graduate from high school, to meet the basic college entrance requirements, to meet private university requirements, and to fulfill requirements for their college major.

Right now is a good time to go back and to review the main points of Chapter 6, "*Think Backwards,*" before you begin strategizing the above four requirements.

For example, look at "Javier," who plans to enter Harvard's Applied Engineering and Sciences program. To graduate from his high school, Javier is only required to complete two years of mathematics (Algebra I being the minimum math level accepted), while the college preparatory requirements for mathematics include three years of math (Algebra II being the minimum math level accepted).

However, Javier would not realistically be a strong candidate for a college engineering program without higher level math. In his strategy, Javier's goal should be to complete AP or IB Calculus prior to graduation (ideally both AB and BC sections).

Even if you are not a math major, in your mind you should be calculating how it would be possible for Javier to complete both AB and BC Calculus sections before graduating. If you quickly backtrack, you know it will require completion of geometry, Algebra II, pre-calculus, Calculus AB, and finally Calculus BC. That's five (5) years of coursework. How's that possible?

Javier used the strategy outlined in Chapter 6, "Think *Backwards*." He bypassed one year of pre-algebra by challenging the curriculum and taking an equivalency examination outlined in Chapter 5, "Work the System." In doing so, he was able to complete geometry in the eighth grade. When he began his freshman year, he was already enrolled in Algebra II.

Another example: Say Marisela plans to major in Chicano/Latino Studies at University of Southern California (USC). At her high school, Marisela is only required to take one year of modern language to fulfill the graduation requirements, while the college preparatory requirements require two years (with three years recommended). However, to be a competitive applicant for USC's program, it would be wise for Marisela to complete four years of Spanish (including AP or IB Spanish) and take the SAT Subject Test in Spanish.

Each situation is different, so create a tailored game plan that reflects your child's unique college goals. The point is to be informed about the *Big Four* before registering for high school.

Maintain an Accelerated Schedule. An accelerated schedule for your middle school student is one in which your student will advance through middle school at a faster rate than his/her peers who follow a traditional schedule. This plan of action will allow your middle school student to bypass curricula so that s/he will have completed some prerequisite high school courses *prior* to entering high school. This strategy is beneficial for students who wish to take the most advanced curriculum available at their high school campus. A detailed explanation, with examples, is found in Chapter 5, "Work the System."

High School. In the third section of this book, Chapter 20, "High School Timelines At a Glance," you will find an outline containing the items your high school student should complete in each school year. However, in this section we will cover a set of strategies that encompass both academic and non-academic activities that will place your child in the most competitive position for college admissions.

If you followed the chapters entitled, "Work the System," "Thinking Backwards," "Ignacia la Ingeniosa," and "Set Up a Game Plan" throughout your child's K-5 and middle school years, then jumping into high school ¡es pan comido!

Focus on GPA, Class Rank, and Rigorous Curriculum. In addition to focusing on the Big Four, your student's main concern should be focusing on GPA (Grade Point Average). To be a competitive college applicant, your student must receive as many "A" grades as possible.

I wish I had a secret strategy to help your student obtain a 4.0 GPA. Unfortunately, I do not. The truth is that obtaining a high GPA is simply a matter of hard work. If your student is willing to put in many hours of study, obtain tutoring if necessary, or join a study group, s/he will greatly increase the chances of raising the GPA.

Your student's GPA is, understandably, one of the most critical factors considered for college admissions. Even if your student cleverly strategizes extracurricular activities, assumes leadership positions at school, and completes 100 hours of community service each year, if his/her GPA is below a 3.0, it will be somewhat challenging to earn admission to college.

Selective colleges and universities will carefully review your student's GPA and class rank. What is class rank? Class rank is a method used by the high school registrar to calculate where your student is "ranked" compared to the rest of the high school class. For example, at Merrill F. West High School, Carlos and Gabi belonged to a senior class of 735 students. A rank of 1/735 would mean that this student had the highest GPA in the senior class.

Many highly selective universities will recruit students from within the top 5 percent of the graduating class. In this scenario, that would mean the students "ranked" in the spots 1 through 36 would belong to the top 5 percent. Keep in mind Ivy League schools will be looking at the *weighted* GPA in considering class rank. This is because the weighted rank considers and factors the Honors, and AP/IB courses (those that are considered the most difficult).

Class rank and rigor of curriculum go hand-in-hand. Selective universities seek students who have challenged themselves with the most rigorous curriculum available. Rigorous curriculum refers to challenging courses such as honors, Advanced Placement (AP), and International Baccalaureate (IB) courses. To determine which courses are available at your student's high school campus, ask a guidance counselor or find an online catalog on the counseling department's webpage.

Also keep in mind that the average admitted student to the *most* selective college campuses will have taken an average of eight (8) AP or IB courses. My own children took 10 AP courses in high school – definitely a big plus for their academic profiles.

This sounds brutal, right? But, the reality is most competitive students will be beefing up their portfolio by enrolling in many AP or IB courses. What if your student's high school campus does not provide a comprehensive AP or IB program? In that case, the universities will not negatively assess the student's profile because the courses were simply not offered. If you'd like tips on how to augment your student's academic portfolio, see my blog articles on my website www.quetzalmama.com.

Strategize college admission related examinations. There is a strategy regarding the timing and preparation for these examinations. See Chapter 14, "College Entrance Exams," for a detailed explanation and strategies for taking the PSAT, SAT/ACT, SAT Subject Matter tests, and AP/IB examinations.

Strategize Extracurricular Activities. While focusing on "The Big Four" and the highest GPA possible, help your student focus on these three areas of extracurricular activities: Leadership, Community Service, and Internships. Review Chapter 13, "Extracurricular Activities."

Leadership. As a college admissions coach, each year it becomes more evident that leadership activities hold a lot of weight compared with other factors. My students with the greatest involvement in leadership activities nearly always outperform their peers with similar GPA's and SAT/ACT scores when it comes to admissions offers.

In the freshman year of high school, ensure your son/daughter becomes a member of an on-campus organization—**preferably a Latino-based organization**. The first year of involvement in this organization will help gain familiarity with the organization's structure, key players, and allow her to demonstrate her leadership skills. When your child becomes a sophomore, s/he will be ready to run for an officer position within this same organization. Perhaps it is Secretary, Treasurer, Public Relations Officer, or even Vice President. Follow this pattern through the senior year of high school. The goal is to become elected to the highest position possible (e.g., President) by the fall of the senior year.

This strategy will convey to the Admissions team three things about your child: (1) s/he is committed to an organization and has the responsibility and discipline to follow through; (2) s/he is highly respected by peers and viewed as a leader, as they have elected your child to an officer position; and (3) s/he is culturally authentic, as this child belongs to an organization that supports pride in ethnic heritage.

What if a particular club of interest does not exist at your son or daughter's high school campus? In this case, your student should propose forming a new club with the site principal or vice principal and obtain bylaws to understand how to begin such a charter.

Other times, a club may have been established at the school site but an advisor is not available to help run the club for a particular school year. In this case, you (the parent) can ask to become the advisor. It will require a background check, and if transportation is required, proof of a valid driver's license and insurance. Check with the site principal, read the bylaws, and help your students overcome any obstacles that may prevent them from participating in leadership positions.

Community Service. Ideally, your student will invest at least 100 hours of community service each year of high school, for a total of 400 hours by the time s/he graduates from high school. Having completed this commendable record of service will enhance the college application process, benefit the community, and provide an avenue for many scholarships. 100 hours per year sounds like a lot; however, if your student completes this service during the summer months, it can be accomplished within a matter of two to three weeks.

A lot of students overlook the opportunity to strategize their community service for maximum effectiveness. For more information on strategizing Community Service, see Chapter 13, "Extracurricular Activities." Once your student has identified a service opportunity, s/he should stick with that program for all four years.

For example, if your son Julio aspires to major in political science at UCLA (with the ultimate goal of attending law school), then Julio should conduct community service related to his academic and career goals. What does that look like? Julio should volunteer for a local political organization that supports the Latino community. For example, he could be a volunteer at the Council for Spanish Speaking or a local MALDEF chapter. In this capacity, Julio gains hands-on experience, has exposure within his chosen field, and helps others within his community. It is a win-win-win!

Here's another example. Say Alejandra aspires to be a Registered Nurse (RN) and will be applying to an impacted nursing program at a selective college. For her community service, she should volunteer at her local clinic or hospital or volunteer for an organization that provides health-related educational services for the Latino community.

Internships. An internship is a summer program (or in some cases throughout the school year) that offers a specific focus (such as medicine, law, etc.) where your student receives exposure to his/her field of study. It may involve a research project, specialized instruction, hands-on training, or various activities. There is often a project goal to be completed at the end of the internship, and sometimes the students will present their project to leaders within their field of study. The internship may be paid or voluntary or short-term (e.g., two weeks) or the entire summer (eight weeks). The program may also be comprised of a team of interns or a single intern.

If your student desires admission to a competitive university, start strategizing summer internships as early as the ninth grade. My website lists internship programs available for high school students; nearly all are specifically geared toward underrepresented students. Some of the national internship programs are highly competitive and provide paid housing, meals, and a cash stipend. Others are regional programs with few applicants and no stipend. Keep in mind an internship can also be an informal program where your student conducts independent re-search with the help of a mentor.

For example, since my daughter Gabi knew she wanted to receive admission into a competitive biological science program, she focused on acquiring an internship each year throughout high school. In the summer of her freshman year, she participated in a medicine-related program at UCLA. In the summer of her sophomore year, she participated in an eight-week paid summer internship at UC San Diego's School of Medicine. Having gained research experience working in a laboratory the two previous summers, she was selected in her junior year to participate in Stanford University's Summer Institute for Medical Research (SIMR). In this summer program, she conducted research in the Neuroscience Institute and was given the privilege of working along-side top neurologists and brain surgeons. It is my belief that the special-ized focus of her summer research programs made her an exceptional candidate for Ivy League admission.

What if you cannot identify a formal internship program in your town or region? In this case your student can do one of two things. S/ he can identify programs outside of your geographic radius or can cre-ate an independent internship program. How so? Many local college professors run a laboratory, have funding for specialized research, or need students to help them with various projects throughout the year.

Your student can contact a local professor and ask for the oppor-tunity to meet in person and to discuss an internship proposal. For example, a political science professor may be conducting a study and needs a student to help organize and to document data. Or, maybe a local biological science professor is conducting research for a book. The professor might need a student or two to help conduct simple laboratory experiments or to collect data.

You can see that there are many, many opportunities to create an internship when one does not exist. The pay or stipend for such an internship is not the goal. The goal is for your student to gain hands-on experience and exposure within the targeted discipline. An internship listed on your student's college application will help the student stand out compared to the other thousands of applicants vying for admission.

What About Sports, You Ask? I am often asked this question from students and their parents. Sports are great! I am a sports advocate with one condition: Can your student easily handle all of the extracurricular activities (leadership, community service, etc.) while maintaining an impressive GPA? If the answer is "Yes," then go for it.

However, sports-related activities are a big investment of time and may take away from precious study hours. My children participated in varsity sports each year throughout high school. However, I carefully monitored their grades to ensure they were on track. If their grades had slipped, they would have been removed from the team. While there are significant scholarships for "star" athletes, unless your student is extremely gifted in a sport, it would be wiser to focus on grades.

CHAPTER 9

NINJA TOOLS FOR LATINA MOMS

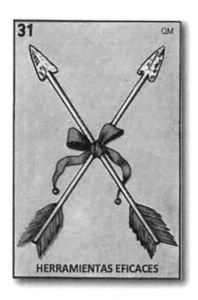

We don't value education.
We are not engaged.
We are deficient.

THE FALSE STATEMENTS above represent myths that have somehow endured through time. These myths flood our classrooms, communities, and the minds of impressionable youth. We experience these myths when we are asked:

Why don't you just attend the PTA Meeting?
(You'd make this a priority if you really cared)

Why don't you volunteer in your child's classroom?
(*I guess you think it is our job to manage your child's academic success*)

Why Don't You Just Learn English?
(We don't value your culture or language. Lose it.)

We Latina moms are told we are deficient in nearly all areas: we don't have the capital to help our students navigate the educational system; we are not vocal or present on campus; we don't have the language or knowledge to help our children succeed; and we don't place a priority on getting our kids to college.

I hear this often. I read it in articles, I hear it from other non-Latino parents, and I see this assumption in research. However, we know this to be untrue and without merit. We *do* value education but we struggle to provide our children with college-going tools because we did not go through the college admission process in the United States. Our child's education *is* a priority but we cannot attend the PTA meetings because we are busy working during the day to support our families. We *do* care about our children very much, and we would volunteer in their class-rooms but we are often made to feel unwelcome and undervalued.

How convenient! This deficit model conveniently allows educa-tional institutions, government policy, and privileged folks to redirect the blame for the lack of Latino students in college, and place it in the lap of us parents. This is a convenient and simplistic way to view the complex and historical issue of the current academic gap in higher education.

You got this, mom! But, this is not a book about victimization and whining. This book is intended to empower parents – to understand our obstacles but work through them with successful strategies. With this positive mindset, I'm here to tell you that we Latina moms have some of the best tools – Ninja tools in fact – to help our children succeed in academics and in life. Let me explain.

Researchers, neuroscientists, and educators are now discovering that a set of student characteristics – **not** income, **not** DNA or IQ, **not** parent's education level – will be the <u>greatest determinant</u> of whether a student enrolls *and* graduates from college. The best part: These characteristics are not set at birth. They can be taught, cultivated, and are malleable *at any age*. The characteristics associated with student success are as follows:

Gratitude

Optimism

Motivation

Curiosity

Zest (enthusiasm & energy)

Self Control/Willpower

Resilience

Grit (aka "Ganas")

We Latino parents have what many parents wish they had: the natural ability to ensure our children are successful in school and in life. Ironically, it is our very life circumstances that have led us to adapt and adopt these successful Ninja traits. These skills are taught and reinforced through our culture, modeled through our behaviors, and exemplified by our historical accomplishments.

We teach our children to feel *grateful*, by teaching them the ability to see the greatness in what we do have, versus our shortcomings.

We teach our children to remain *optimistic*, despite the many negative issues that may infiltrate our homes, work places, schools, and communities.

We teach our children to remain *motivated*, even though there are many de-motivating forces that surround them.

We foster *curiosity* by encouraging our children to figure things out independently.

The *energy and enthusiasm* our children possess is the direct result of our daily encouragement. We teach them to embrace the day with vigor and resilience.

The last three traits – self-control/willpower, resilience, and grit (ganas), will be discussed separately because I feel these traits are most closely aligned with getting our kids to college.

Self Control/Willpower – To introduce the characteristic "Self Control/Willpower" I must first introduce the famous Marshmallow Test. The Marshmallow Test was an experiment by psychologist Walter Mischel at Stanford University, testing delayed gratification in children during the late 60's and early 70's.

A child was offered a choice between an immediate reward (one marshmallow) or given the option to wait (delay) for a short period of time while the researcher left the room and later returned. If the student waited those 15 minutes, s/he would be given two marshmallows instead of one – double the rewards. The research team found that those children who could wait longer had better life outcomes including higher scores on standardized exams, higher educational attainment, better health and other positive outcomes.

So, what does this Marshmallow Test have to do with Latino parents? How can we use this theory to help increase odds of getting our own children into college? I'd like to share three, simple, no-cost strategies you can employ right now to help your children learn and embrace delayed gratification. All three of these strategies are related to the Marshmallow theory:

Putting Money in the Bank. Putting money in the bank is a metaphor to help our children visualize how short-term, specific tasks accumulate as an "investment" toward long-term future goals. In our house, it works like this. When my kids are engaging in a non-productive activity, or putting off an exercise or homework assignment, I ask them which activity puts money in their bank? I motion my hand in the direction of my coat pocket to illustrate this visually.

I rhetorically ask, "Which activity puts money in your bank? What choice will you make right now to positively impact your future?" I want them to acknowledge how the choices they make today have great influence over tomorrow. The bottom line is to have them engage in a mental activity to reinforce the connection between making an immediate choice and a long-term payout. This self-control/willpower strategy helps them understand the "*why.*"

One-On-One Exchange. For every chunk of time your children spend on a designated activity – whether it's one minute or one hour – they reward themselves with an equivalent amount of time on a different activity they pick. For example, one hour of chess can be exchanged for one hour of watching their favorite movie. Or, one hour of reading is equivalent to one hour of playing video games. The activity they choose as their "reward" should be non-material – nothing consumer driven that requires a visit to ToysRUs or Game Stop. This psychological activity is effective because it is both logical and democratic. Kids understand the rationale and feel empowered to make their own choices. You set the parameters and they pick how they will reward themselves. This self-control/willpower exercise teaches the "*how.*"

First Thing / First Priority. As soon as your kids get home from school, the "first thing" or first priority is to prioritize the list of homework activities for the day and begin work immediately. This means a school-related assignment will always come first in your house before any other task, chore, or leisure activity. School related assignments include homework, reading, research, studying for an exam, or attending tutoring sessions. To implement this in your home, it must be a family commitment where everyone is on board. This self-control/willpower exercise teaches kids about the "*when*."

Delayed gratification is challenging. And, the marshmallow theory is tricky with kids and college admissions. Why? Because we're asking our kindergartner, 4th grader, or middle schooler to look into the very distant future while making sacrifices now. For a 2nd grader, that's 10 years of delayed gratification! We want our kids to see the "light at the end of the tunnel" so they are not overwhelmed by the daunting goal of college admission.

The key is to break up this long period of time into manageable segments. For K-5 students, have your kids visualize the goal of maintaining strong grades in order to qualify for a desired magnet middle school program (short-term). For middle school kids, have your kids visualize successful completion of middle school prerequisite honors English, math, or science courses to qualify for desired placement in more challenging high school curriculum.

Resilience –Resilience is defined as the ability to recover readily from adversity, set-backs, challenges, and obstacles. Latino parents wrote the bible on how to develop resilience in our kids. We Latinos have been enculturated with this positive trait and have mastered it to a science. We teach our children how to pick themselves up when they are not successful. We show our children how to maneuver around set-backs and obstacles. We tell them to anticipate road blocks, but to remain courageous and determined.

When our children are required to experience and navigate through adversity, challenges, obstacles, and hardship, they develop *resilience.* Why and how is resilience related to college admissions? Because, the trait of resilience is closely aligned with the challenges our students will encounter throughout their undergraduate and graduate education. These challenges may be physical, mental, or psychological. Students who give up easily, who adapt a defeatist attitude, and who succumb to pressures, will not thrive in a competitive college environment.

While there is no "test" for resilience, it will be clear on your student's college application whether or not they have mastered this trait. It will be gleaned through the rigorous courses they enrolled, from their sustained stamina and longevity in extracurricular activities, and from their overall academic success. Combined with being situated in a low-resourced school, it will be obvious resilience was a significant factor that aided the student in overcoming many hurdles. Interestingly, the adversity and challenges our Latino students experience will transform into positive life adaptation skills that sets them up for success in college.

Grit (aka *Ganas*) – As a college admissions expert, I believe *Ganas* is the most valuable college-going trait we can instill in our children. In fact, I wrote an entire chapter entitled, "*The Ganas Principle*" in my book, "Nailed It!" I saved this trait for last because I want to emphasize the importance of Latino parents modelling this skill, behavior, and mindset. Interestingly, it is student's responses to failure (not success) that researchers are now touting as the golden ticket to success.

This trait is similar to the trait "resilience," but slightly different. While resilience helps our children recover from situations and endure adversity, *Ganas* is a pre-emptive strategy. *Ganas* requires initiative and drive – making it a proactive mindset, whereas resilience is reactive.

It's that voice inside that hollers, "I think I can do this. I'm going for it!" *Ganas* is a forward thinking mindset, inspired by optimistic thinking and positive visualization of future goals, whereas *Resilience* is how we remain on our pathway toward those goals.

In general, Latino parents may cultivate the eight traits above by practicing the following strategies to help their children succeed amidst obstacles encountered in K-5, middle school, and throughout high school. Some of these strategies include:

- Encouraging your child to embrace and deal with set-backs and challenges (not shielding them from adversity).
- Helping your child cognitively separate the challenge or set-back versus personally identifying with the struggle in a negative, self-attributing way.
- Encouraging your child to view obstacles as a "gift" that will enable positive growth.
- Helping your student delay gratification by incorporating routines that yield a "payout" for self-discipline.

Learning about these eight traits is empowering for Latino parents because it validates what we are *already* doing, practicing, encouraging, modelling, and exemplifying with our children.

It means our current Ninja practices have high value, and will positively influence the direction and success of our child's pathway to college. It means our children are equipped with the tools to set optimistic goals, remain focused, maneuver through difficult challenges, and cross the finish line with gratitude.

CHAPTER 10

GET REAL

16 QM

HAY QUE SER REALISTA

NO TEACHER BEGINS her day by formulating a plan to discriminate intentionally against our Latino students. No teacher in America wakes up each morning and says: "Today, I'm going to view Asian students as superior in math and view Latino students as lazy and dumb. I will give preference and attention only to white students. I will prevent Latino students from advancing in all subjects, make them feel inadequate, and create obstacles so that Latino students cannot reach their full academic potential."

Hopefully this example illustrates how ridiculous it would be to believe all white teachers consciously and intentionally behave in ways to make our Latino children fail.

However, it would also be ridiculous to say discrimination (whether intentional or unintentional) does not exist in our classrooms. It should be noted that today 82% of public school teachers in America are white, whereas in California 53% of students attending public schools are Latino.

We are not in a post-racial era, and we are not colorblind. Research still proves one of the first things we humans notice is not your smile or shoes but the color of your skin, eyes, and ethnicity. If we were truly in a post-racial society where every student was judged and valued based on merit, you would not be reading this book—nor would I have been compelled to write it.

The litmus test to determine whether or not we live in a post-racial era is when Latino, African-American, and Native American parents are no longer required to give their kids "the talk."

The Talk – You know "the talk." The talk is that dreaded conversation many Latino parents have with their pre-school-aged children as they enter a K-5 school system. The talk is our cautionary warning to prepare our children for what they will undoubtedly encounter in school—to be diligent in the classroom, to defend their work, to be given proper credit, and not to be overlooked or bypassed for academic opportunities.

The talk will mention how their teachers and administrators may view them differently and how to prepare them for overcoming negative bias and stereotypes.

This is the conversation my husband and I had with all three of our children, and we know (sadly) our conversation is probably very similar to conversations other Latino parents have with their children. Just as the parents reading this book, we also want the best for our children. We believe it is crucial our children are not misguided as they enter the K-5 institution because we know some of the inevitable things they will experience—the same things we experienced and our parents experienced.

It is one of the most difficult conversations you will have with your child because it tells your child in one brief conversation that (1) The world views Latino children differently; (2) Meritocracy is a lie; and (3) In addition to their normal school workload, they will also have an additional burden to overcome.

While you do not want your child to feel there is a big conspiracy out there—conspiring for his/her failure—you need to inform your child of the reality of the world in which we live. As parents, my husband and I always believed that being prepared, knowing all of our obstacles, and being proactive would be a better approach for our three children than giving them excuses. Our children, like yours, are bright and ask a lot of questions. If your children are not prepared and experience negative interactions in school that have nothing to do with their abilities, they will be confused.

Whether or not you choose to have "the talk" with your children is something you will need to discuss and carefully decide. If you choose to be pro-active and inform your children, it is critical that this be done in a positive and empowering way. The goal is to help your child become psychologically prepared to deal positively and effectively with racism rather than internalize negative feelings or create self-hatred.

Not taking this concept lightly, I naturally conducted research to ensure my strategy was sound. I was reassured to find that informing children, rather than shielding them from the truth, is a better long-term psychological strategy. For example, in his book, "Beyond the Big Test: Noncognitive Assessment in Higher Education," Dr. William Sedlacek addresses how a student's understanding of racism and academic performance go hand-in-hand: *"Research has consistently shown that students of color who understand racism and are prepared to deal with it perform better academically."*

Dr. Gloria G. Rodriguez, author of *Raising Nuestros Niños*, also recommends that Latino parents discuss the topic of racial discrimination openly with their children:

> You should sensitize your children very early in life to the fact that discrimination and racism are still alive and that they may be victims of it. Encourage your children to discuss issues related to discrimination, whether they be incidents they have experienced or problems of the world that need to be addressed with more mutual respect, compassion, and cooperation. Teach your children to speak up against hate and discrimination.

I do not believe every white person is racist or that no white person has your child's best interest at heart. But, I will say it again: I live in the real world. I became real years ago when my kids began experiencing subtle (and not so subtle) acts of discrimination, racism, and plain neglect. Unfortunately, I have numerous personal examples to verify the unfortunate truth of living in the "real" world. These examples range from my daughter being threatened by an administrator for being a "gang member," my son being interrogated by a team of adults as to whether his Science Fair entry was truly his own and not written by an adult (or someone who, presumably, was more knowledgeable), and the constant doubt that my kids earned admission to college based on merit.

Most recently, when our daughter gained admission to every Ivy League university, many persons questioned (to my face) whether she was admitted through merit or through "Affirmative Action." I reminded these individuals that there does not exist a separate "Affirmative Action" scoring method by The College Board (the company that administers the SAT and Advanced Placement exams), or a separate "Affirmative Action" grading curve by our School Registrar (our daughter was Valedictorian).

One individual said, "Hmm. I wonder *what* it is about your daughter that makes her *so special?*" This individual was alluding to special treatment she believed Gabi received as a "minority" candidate. I reminded this person that Gabi received admission because of her stellar SAT and AP exam scores, Valedictorian status, being named National Hispanic Scholar and AP Scholar with Honor, four years of scientific research (including being published in a medical journal by 17 years of age), Captain of the Varsity Tennis Team, 400 hours of community service, President of the Pre-Med Club and MEChA Club, and numerous national awards for academics.

Although these are reasonable factors that most persons would agree make a highly qualified college applicant, I knew my information fell on deaf ears. The truth is, if a non-Latino student with these same qualifications received admission to selective universities, the assumption would be the student earned their spot.

I am not including this information to rile up your sense of injustice. I am simply reminding Latino parents that it is our job to be diligent so our children are prepared to handle these situations. Throughout all of these humiliating situations, my children knew to expect (but not accept) these marginalizations and how to handle these types of encounters. When our children are prepared, they can focus their attention on their goal of obtaining a quality education.

Getting real doesn't mean becoming a militant parent, defensively awaiting any slight, or anticipating discrimination around every corner. It means you cannot believe discrimination is a thing of the past, that our society is now color blind, or that all persons have your Latino child's best interests at heart. I encourage all Latino parents to "get real" with institutionalized racism in a pro-active way so that our children will become empowered students on their way to college.

Getting real means accepting there are individuals and systems in place that have the potential to rob your Latino child of an *equal* education. If you are intimidated by the dominant group or do not want to "cause waves," you need to get over it. **Your kids need for you to be real.**

CHAPTER 11

AVE ENJAULADA

WHETHER IT IS fear, anxiety, or lack of understanding of the college system, many devoted Latino parents discourage their daughters from attending college far away from home. It doesn't happen often with our male students, but it is prevalent with females. Because the majority of students I coach are Latina (approximately 80%), I watch this tragedy play out each year. Sadly, every year I learn that a top student who earned admission to an excellent campus has been told by her parents she cannot attend a particular college because it is too far from home.

No matter the student's academic profile or the exceptional financial aid packages offered (typically a "full ride"), these Latina students feel trapped – placed in a no-win situation. They truly wish to follow their dreams, actualize their potential, and earn a spot at a university aligned with their intellect and career goals. Yet, if they pursue that path, they will disobey their parents and risk being ostracized by their family.

Unfortunately, by discouraging or refusing to support our daughter's decision to attend a non-local or out-of-state college, we may unwittingly deprive them of a lifetime of rewards. Our daughters are often asked to give up exceptional financial aid packages, relinquish their college dream that likely began in elementary school, forfeit an opportunity to thrive in an academic institution surrounded by intellectual peers, and give up being the person they have worked hard to become.

I know Latino parents are not being selfish or punitive. They simply fear the unknown, worry that their daughters won't be safe, and lack an understanding of how different types of colleges will have different outcomes. For this reason, I felt compelled to write this chapter. Speaking of safety, did you know you can find crime statistics for every college at the College Navigator site? Find stats here: https://nces.ed.gov/collegenavigator

Trust me, you don't want your daughter to run away from home as the only option to pursue her college dreams (true story). And, you don't want to place your daughter in a position where she must solicit help from other adults or strangers in order to work through the application process.

Parents ask me, *"What's so bad about attending a local university or community college? Aren't all colleges the same? Isn't the point to just get a degree?"*

No. All colleges are *not* equal. Below are three critical factors that can significantly impact your daughter's ability to be succeed in college, to leave college without a lot of debt, and to graduate on time – or graduate at all, from college.

Limited Financial Aid. Many colleges differ greatly in terms of their sources of financial aid. Public institutions generally receive funding from the state or other governmental entities, whereas private institutions generally rely on income from private donations, organizations, and student tuition. Sometimes aid is restricted to financial *need*, not merit. This means that some colleges may not have discretionary funds to recruit top students or to offer financial "perks."

On the other hand, some universities have discretionary funds to offer exceptional financial aid packages to top students based on *merit*. They tend to have the highest endowments so they can afford offering "full rides" or near full rides. Their financial aid is not restricted to financial need so they can provide 'merit' based incentives to students with exceptional academic performance.

Here are a few examples of highly resourced universities that offer exceptional financial aid to admitted students:

Harvard University
Families with total income less than $65,000
are not expected to contribute.
Families between $65,000 and $150,000
will contribute 0-10% of income

Stanford University
Families with total income less than $65,000
are not expected to contribute.
Families with Income Less than 125,000 Pay ZERO Tuition

University of California "Blue & Gold Program"
Families with Income Less Than $80,000 Pay ZERO Tuition

Bottom line: Compare award letters side by side to understand how much out-of-pocket expenses your family will incur over four years. See the tools at the end of this chapter to help your family make an informed decision regarding the costs of attending a particular college.

Low Graduation Rates. Your daughter's success at the local university or community college can be impacted by the campus' graduation rates. I highly encourage parents to review graduation rates for all colleges being considered – including community colleges. The Department of Education provides a College Scorecard that lists the graduation rates of all colleges in the U.S. Find it here: collegescorecard.ed.gov/.

Too Long to Graduate. If you identify a college with solid graduation rates, it's also important to know, on average, *how long* it takes students to earn a four-year Bachelor's Degree. You might be surprised to learn that some local colleges have an average of *six to eight years* for their students to complete a Bachelor's Degree.

These low rates mean your daughter's chances of graduating in less than six years are low, and graduating in four years is even lower. Because it may take her longer to graduate, she will be paying significantly more over the years to cover the additional tuition, fees, transportation costs, and books. Additionally, she will likely forfeit years of potential annual salary – due to remaining in college additional years versus working in a career. Oh, and some state aid ceases after four years, not six years.

To be fair, compare your daughter's prospective out-of-state or non-local graduation rates with the local campus(es). For example, in 2014, 93% of females graduated from UCLA in six years or less, and more than 80% of all students earned their bachelor's degree in four years. Or, read the U.S. News & World Report's "Highest 4 Year Graduation Rates" to find graduation rates for colleges you are considering. On that list, you will find that some colleges have an 88% to 93% graduation rate within four years.

Hopefully you can see that if we insist our daughters stay close to home, we are asking them to risk graduating on time (or at all), to incur substantial debt to make up for the additional years to graduate, to give up lucrative financial aid packages, and to settle for a campus misaligned with their college and career goals.

Now, Quetzal Mama doesn't just talk the talk. My own daughter received admission to several local campuses including Stanford University and UC Berkeley (both within driving distance to our home). However, Gabi's dream was to experience the East Coast and attend an Ivy League institution. That was her dream since she was five years old. She worked hard to achieve her dream of attending an Ivy League college. I could not clip her wings.

When the time came, Gabi declared she would attend Harvard University. Instead of demanding that she accept the outstanding local offers of admission, our entire family celebrated her decision and encouraged her to soar. It wasn't easy and I won't tell you I didn't cry on occasion when I walked past her bedroom before going to sleep. She's our only daughter (we have two sons). But, let's remember the definition of a Quetzal Mama:

> *A Quetzal Mama is a proud Latina mom who will do anything to ensure her children fulfill their chosen path. A Quetzal knows her children have unique gifts and talents and will make a profound contribution to society. As such, a Quetzal Mama provides her children with every opportunity for success and removes all barriers.*

Having read the above, there is no contingency that your children follow their path *as long as that path is within driving distance to you!* Of course, you will miss your son or daughter if they enroll in a college far from home. We missed Gabi tremendously. However, as a Quetzal Mama I knew Gabi's path included Harvard University—which, incidentally, was 3,147.85 miles from our home in California! But who's counting?

Having read this chapter, I'm hoping you can understand that if we clip our daughter's wings we are locking them in a metaphorical cage. We are silencing their dreams and aspirations. We are asking our daughters to pay a big price for our insecurities and fear. We are overlooking the long-term benefits of our child attending a higher re-sourced campus with greater odds of success. However, parents can be reassured by these insightful words from a few Latino parents:

"Even when birds fly – birds always return home, season after season."

"You have to let her spread her wings.
Success won't happen if she's kept in the nest forever."

Here is a list of helpful tools to guide parents and students in their decision making process. These tools are from repu-table organizations and provide up-to-date information:

College Affordability & Transparency Center
(The Department of Education)
How much you can expect to pay.
Colleges with highest/lowest tuition & fees.
http://collegecost.ed.gov/

Net Price Calculator
All colleges receiving federal fund-ing must publish the true costs

of attending their university and it must
be posted on their website.
Find all net price calculators here:
collegecost.ed.gov/netpricecenter.aspx

College Scorecard
Graduation rates of all colleges in the U.S.
collegescorecard.ed.gov

College Results (Comparison Tool)
Compare net costs, graduation rates, and much more.
collegeresults.org

THE COLLEGE APPLICATION PROCESS

PART THREE FOCUSES *exclusively* on preparing students for the college application. You'll learn how to help your student in the freshman, sophomore, junior, and senior year of high school.

Course Selection
Extracurricular Activities
College Entrance Exams
Letters of Recommendation
Early Action versus Regular Decision
The Personal Statement
How to Select the Right College
The College Interview
High School Timelines at a Glance
Think You're Ready to Apply?

CHAPTER 1 2

COURSE SELECTION

IN PREVIOUS CHAPTERS you learned how to pick the right high school campus and map out four years of high school using the strategy in Chapter 6 (Think *Backwards*). In this section, you'll learn *what types of classes* your student should enroll based on their college aspirations.

Let me share a story now. A few years ago, a student called me to ask my opinion on her odds of getting into Stanford. She triumphantly declared she held a 4.0 GPA and therefore felt she was right on track for admission to Stanford. However, when I read her transcript I was confused. Yes, she indeed had a 4.0 GPA. However, she neglected to take a single Honors or AP course. Naturally, I asked if her school offered any such courses. She said they had plenty of AP courses, but she opted *not* to take them because she was scared it would lower her GPA.

Unfortunately, the student did not get into Stanford (or any other competitive university). However, if she had received coaching even two years earlier, her outcome may have been significantly different. Moral of this story? A student should never compromise the rigor of his/her course work by taking less challenging courses to increase his/her GPA. For this reason, I included this chapter to help your student avoid this tragic mistake.

Course Selection – So, let's talk about the importance of course selection. When selecting high school curriculum, all courses are *not* equal. Admissions officers will be looking at your student's GPA *and* the rigor of his/her curricula. This is especially important for students considering selective colleges.

When scanning your student's transcript, Admission Officers will be especially interested in the Honors, AP, or IB courses taken. These courses are *weighted* (given extra points) because they are more challenging compared to traditional courses. Therefore, selective colleges expect to see rigorous coursework on the applicant's transcript.

Why? The most obvious reason to take rigorous curriculum is because colleges are interested in students who have challenged themselves to the best of their abilities. Second, they seek students who are passionate about learning. Most importantly, taking AP or IB courses demonstrates a student's ability to succeed in a rigorous curriculum – a college admission benchmark to determine whether a student may or may not thrive at their campus.

How many AP or IB courses do competitive candidates complete? To answer this question, let's look at UCLA's most recently admitted class (2015). The majority of **admitted students** enrolled in 16 to 20 semesters of Honors or AP courses. That means the majority of admitted students took between 8 and 10 AP or IB courses. The students I coach typically take 8 to 10 AP courses.

But, here's the tricky part. While we want our students to take challenging courses, we don't want them to risk lowering the GPA by taking courses that might be *too challenging*. How does your student balance this? The following questions will help determine which subjects and how many AP or IB courses to take.

- Is the course(s) aligned with your student's discipline? For example, if your student intends to major in Human Biology, then it makes sense they take AP Biology or AP Chemistry, right? Or, if the student intends to declare Journalism or English as a major, then we'd expect the student to take AP English. If your student's transcript does not reflect coursework related to the major, it will raise a red flag.

- Even if the course is not "over their head," will your student's involvement in the course place an undue hardship (homework assignments, additional study hours, etc.)? Your student should interview other students to learn about the expected workload from a particular teacher/class.

- Does your student attend a high school campus that is considered exceptionally competitive? Is it likely the course roster will be populated with students within the top 1% of the class? We don't want grade curving that may unfairly compromise your student's GPA.

Bottom line: If your student can handle the rigor of AP, IB, or Honors course(s), they should focus time and energy on earning the highest grade in these courses and in selecting courses aligned with their major.

Know the "Big Four" Requirements. I'm bringing back the "Big Four" to remind parents there are *four* concurrent strategies throughout high school. See Chapter 8, "Set Up a Game Plan." When selecting coursework, keep in mind the curriculum should be aligned with your student's college aspirations.

For example, if your student intends to pursue a less selective state school, then they won't be concerned with private or competitive college requirements. However, even at some state schools, particular majors are impacted. This means the campus will expect students to meet and exceed certain coursework for the major.

And, regardless of whether your student pursues a highly competitive college or a less selective state school, know that they must complete all college preparatory coursework in order to be eligible for these colleges. See Chapter 8, "*Set Up a Game Plan*" (A-G Requirements).

Recap: There are four simultaneous strategies your student should follow to maximize options for college admission:

The Big Four
(Four Simultaneous Strategies)

Graduation Requirements
College Preparatory Requirements
Private or Competitive College Requirements
Discipline-Specific (College Major) Requirements

A side note on AP, IB, or Honors coursework. Some campuses – such as charter schools or low-resourced high schools may not offer comprehensive AP or IB programs. What to do? First, know that a university will not discriminate against your student's inability to take such coursework if their high school did not offer these types of programs. In other words, your student will not be penalized because the classes were unavailable to them. However, there are three (3) strategies to offset this deficiency. Learn more about these strategies by hosting a Quetzal Mama workshop at your middle school or high school! See the Closing chapter for more information to host a workshop in your community.

CHAPTER 13

EXTRACURRICULAR ACTIVITIES

DON'T SKIP THIS chapter! Before you read my strategies on selecting extracurricular activities, I want you to know one thing. I want you to know that all things being equal (grades, test scores, etc.), my students who carefully planned extracurricular activities had greater success in admission to the most selective colleges.

Through the years I've coached thousands of high school students. When viewing their extracurricular profiles it's immediately clear which students planned out activities and which did not. It's also clear which students succumbed to pitfalls such as the "Cover all Bases" or the "Passive" approach. Let's examine these pitfalls before we introduce successful strategies.

"Cover All Bases" – refers to parents who push their students to participate in *every* type of activity. Because these parents are uncertain as to which area to focus, they encourage their students to participate in *everything*. Unfortunately, these parents have made the mistake of believing their child will catch the attention of Admissions Officers if they are involved in every academic, athletic, and community service program. In desperately hoping their student will appear "well rounded" they encourage their children to load up as many extracurricular activities as possible.

Consequently, these student profiles lack a consistent theme, purpose, or direction. They lose sight of the reason why admissions officers want to see these activities on an application: *where their passion lies!* Admissions officers want to know what really matters to the student outside of the classroom. If the student is involved in 50 activities, how does this demonstrate an interest or passion for any single activity?

The "Passive" approach, on the other hand, represents the other extreme. This approach represents students who passively engage in extracurricular opportunities without critical examination. For example, they will only pursue activities advertised in their high school counseling center, those that caught their attention on a posted flyer, or those that their friends have pursued. There is no thought or strategy in a passive approach, and this will be clear in their application.

Now that we know the pitfalls of non-strategic extracurricular activity planning, let's learn how to be strategic in planning our activities. I recommend four (4) strategies:

- Exemplify Quality versus Quantity
- Be Politically Savvy
- Demonstrate Cultural Authenticity
- Focus on Discipline-Specific Activities

Quality Versus Quantity – College Admission officers generally agree in the old adage of *quality over quantity.* What does quality look like? A general rule of thumb: Focus on a few unique activities, consistently over time, with dedication.

For example, consider a student who volunteers every year (possibly since eighth grade or earlier) organizing a fundraiser for a domestic violence shelter. In addition to helping organize this annual event, this student also volunteers during the school year and summer as a tutor at this shelter. Focusing on this singular activity demonstrates the student is focused, passionate, and dedicated to helping women and children.

Be Politically Savvy – A good rule of thumb when strategizing your student's extracurricular activities is to consider what demographic or population the organization serves, who funds the organization, and how the organization is perceived historically? Stay away from organizations that promote a negative or fringe political position or are historically recognized as being associated with one. Another good rule of thumb is to consider humanitarian organizations that advocate for any of the following:

- Domestic Violence
- Educational Empowerment
- Environment
- Homeless Populations
- Immigrant Rights
- Medical Conditions (cancer, etc.)
- Mental or Physical Disabilities
- Socioeconomically Disadvantaged
- Women and Children

The above issues have broad appeal. A great example of a politically neutral organization, with broad appeal and a historically positive reputation in our society, is the Boys and Girls Clubs of America.

There's a Fine Line – Compare the mission of the above broad-appeal organizations to activities linked to politically controversial topics such as abortion, same sex marriage, capital punishment, or firearms. Is the organization considered non-inclusive, militant, ultra conservative, sexist, racist, or elitist?

I'm not suggesting a student fabricate or embellish his/her application when listing extracurricular activities. I'm suggesting that the student understand how their involvement may be perceived from an admissions perspective.

On the other hand, the admissions office may welcome such a student with non-traditional or controversial views. There is a fine line between a student who challenges the status quo or defends non-traditional views, and the student who is perceived as self-righteous, closed minded, lacks empathy, and refuses to embrace diversity and inclusion.

For example, if a student lists on her application she is a chapter representative for The Coalition for Humane Immigrant Rights of Los Angeles (CHIRLA), she will likely be perceived positively, as a social justice advocate. However, if a student lists volunteering for The Council of Conservative Citizens (an organization that supports white nationalism and separatism) the Admissions officer may have a different view.

Demonstrate Cultural Authenticity – Competitive universities want to attract students who bring diversity to their campus. Therefore, they are looking for *culturally authentic* students who will bring a unique voice to their student body. My definition of Cultural Authenticity in a college admissions context follows:

> *Cultural Authenticity refers to the quality a student possesses that represents positive, strong, and consistent affiliation within a cultural group. This quality is based on authentic life experiences within the culture and examples may include religion, politics, language, traditions, and historical knowledge.*
>
> —*Quetzal Mama*

Let's compare two fictitious students to best understand how Cultural Authenticity is articulated in a college application context.

"*Omar*" is President of Moviemiento Estudiantil Chicano de Aztlán (MEChA) at his high school campus. For three consecutive years, Omar has organized a fundraising event to benefit the Coalition for Humane

Immigrant Rights of Los Angeles. Lastly, Omar holds a leadership position in the Society of Hispanic Engineers (SHPE).

Omar's overall set of life experiences (evidenced by his participation
in these activities) will offer his future university a unique voice in their
classrooms—adding positive value for all of their student body. Growing
up in a Latino community Omar intimately understands Latino culture
and politics. He embraces our traditions, language, food, and history.
Most importantly, Omar *positively* identifies belonging to this cultural
group.

Compare Omar to "*Benjamin*" who is a senior at an all-white, private
high school. Benjamin has grown up in a neighborhood where he is the
only Latino, and all of his friends are white. Benjamin identifies with
the dominant group, his family does not practice Latino traditions, his
political affiliation is not aligned with Latino concerns, he is not aware
of the social and historical significance of being Latino, and has limited
exposure to Latino culture. All of his life experiences have been consistent with the dominant group. Most importantly, Benjamin does not
positively identify with being Latino and may have a negative view of his
fellow Latinos.

When Benjamin steps foot on a college campus, his voice will be
indistinguishable from the majority of his fellow freshman. Colleges are
not looking for a homogenous group of entering freshman. They want
students who can bring a unique set of experiences and wisdom into
their classrooms.

Benjamin does not need to come from a high socioeconomic group
or attend a private school (although this may be the case). Intellectually,
Benjamin comprehends he is Latino but does not psychologically view
himself as Latino. He considers himself "different." The fact Benjamin
has Latino ancestry is the only similarity he has with his Latino brothers.

There is a distinction between belonging (by birth and not by choice) to a particular ethnic group or race and *personally identifying* (by choice) with this particular ethnic group or race. The difference is in the student's perception of who s/he is, in how the student views the world, and in the activities which s/he chooses to engage. In other words, the student who personally and positively identifies as being Latino is *culturally authentic*.

There is no box on the Common Application that asks, "Are you culturally authentic?" However, universities can easily distinguish those who are and those who are not. One of the obvious distinguishing factors will be discerned through the list of extracurricular activities. In other words, checking the box on a college application next to "Hispanic/Latino" does not inform the admission readers that the student will bring diversity to the campus.

Focus on Discipline-Specific Activities – Students often overlook the importance of pursuing extracurricular activities related to their academic pursuits. For example, if Maribel is pursuing a chemical engineering major she should become involved in activities related to chemical engineering. Examples might include a summer internship through Stanford's RISE program (Raising Interest in Science and Engineering), membership in Latinas in STEM, the Society of Women Engineers (SWE), Science Olympiad team, Mathematics Engineering Science Achievement (MESA), or Society of Hispanic Professional Engineers (SHPE).

Likewise, if Javier is pursuing a journalism major, his extracurricular activities should include writing for his school newspaper, having membership in a literary club, and serving as an editor of a Latino-based publication. If such activities do not exist at his school campus or community, he can found and organize such an organization (see section on "Leadership" in Chapter 8, "*Set Up a Game Plan*").

Sample Four-Year Plan (Extracurricular Activities)

The following illustrates how "Maribel" tailored her extracurricular activities to demonstrate all four points covered in this chapter. Maribel's activities demonstrate focused, consistent, strategic activities (Quality versus Quantity), aligned with politically positive affiliations (Be Politically Savvy), show involvement in Latino organizations (Demonstrate Cultural Authenticity), and identifies her passion for engineering (Focus on Discipline-Specific Activities).

MARIBEL'S FRESHMAN YEAR:

- Chairperson - MEChA Community Service
- Member - Academic Decathlon and Science Olympiad
- Summer Tutor (100 hours) - Boys and Girls Club
- Member - Folklorico Dance Troupe "Xochipilli"
- Intern - Society of Professional Hispanic Engineers (SHPE)
- Member - MESA

MARIBEL'S SOPHOMORE YEAR:

- Secretary - MEChA
- Member - Academic Decathlon & Science Olympiad
- Summer Tutor (100 hours) - Boys and Girls Club
- Member - Folklorico Dance Troupe "Xochipilli"
- Intern - Society of Professional Hispanic Engineers (SHPE)
- Member - MESA

Maribel's Junior Year:

- Vice President - MEChA
- Member - Academic Decathlon & Science Olympiad
- Summer Tutor (100 hours) - Boys and Girls Club
- Member - Folklorico Dance Troupe "Xochipilli"
- Intern - NASA Summer Institute in Engineering and Computer Applications
- Member - MESA

Maribel's Senior Year:

- President- MEChA
- Semi-Finalist - Siemens Math and Science Competition
- Member - Academic Decathlon and Science Olympiad
- Summer Tutor (100 hours) - Boys and Girls Club
- Member - Folklorico Dance Troupe "Xochipilli"
- Intern - Smithsonian Latino Center, Young Ambassadors Program
- Member - MESA

As you can see, Maribel focused *consistently* on **culturally authentic** activities (MEChA, folklorico), chose **politically savvy** community service (Boys and Girls Club), and focused on **discipline-specific** activities (Siemens Math and Science Competition, Science Olympiad, MESA). Maribel strategized her activities demonstrating **quality over quantity**.

Remember, college admission teams will be looking at Maribel's activities and accomplishments only through the first semester of her senior year of high school. This means your student must have strategically formalized a plan to present the most competitive profile by that time.

A word of caution! The extent to which your student will be involved in extracurricular activities must be balanced with his/her Grade Point Average (GPA). If your student's GPA begins to falter, the extracurricular activities should be suspended until you see grade improvement. Remember, GPA is extremely important. Your student should not compromise GPA for extracurricular activities.

CHAPTER 14

COLLEGE ENTRANCE EXAMS

BEFORE BEGINNING THIS chapter, I want to say a few words about college entrance exams. I'm not a fan of standardized tests for college because they have been proven, time and time again, they are *not* an accurate assessment tool for *aptitude*. Instead, they're best at accurately gaging the income and educational level of the student's parents. Yet, these exams are used to weed out candidates for spots at competitive universities so Latino parents need to be informed about these exams.

Let me share some recent stats to give you an idea of national averages for all students and Latino students:

2015 National Average for *all* US Students
ACT 21
SAT 1490

2015 National Average for *Latino* Students
ACT 18.9
SAT 1343

But, you don't care about national averages, right? You want to know what scores will get your students into the best universities in America, right? Below are some general ranges to give you a glimpse into the world of competitive college entrance exam scores. Keep in mind two things. First, these scores represent some of the most competitive campuses in the US. Second, these numbers are only part of the mix of factors that admissions officers consider when making admission decisions.

Campus	Average SAT*	Average ACT
Harvard University	2120 (low) to 2400 (high)	32 (low) to 35 (high)
Stanford University	2070 (low) to 2350 (high)	31 (low) to 34 (high)
UC Berkeley	1840 (low) to 2240 (high)	27 (low) to 33 (high)

*SAT scores above are based on a rubric phased out Spring 2016.
The new SAT rubric will be based on a total of 1600 points.*

The above scores represent the bottom 25% of admitted students ("low") to the top 75th percentile ("high") of admitted students. To learn strategies to identify college campuses within your student's academic profile, see Chapter 18, "*How to Select the Right College.*" Now, let's look at PreACT and PSAT exams.

PreACT – the ACT will launch their new exam called the "PreACT" beginning Fall 2016. This new exam will allow 10th graders to take this assessment so they can prepare for the experience (and their future performance) on the actual ACT.

PSAT – The formal name of this examination is the *Preliminary SAT/National Merit Scholarship Qualifying Test.* The acronym is the PSAT/NMSQT or, more commonly, the PSAT. The PSAT is administered through the College Board and the National Merit Scholarship Corporation (NMSC).

The PSAT/NMSQT is a "preliminary" examination to help students prepare for the SAT. The PSAT measures three areas: (1) critical reading skills; (2) math problem-solving skills; and (3) writing skills. In the fall of your student's sophomore year (tenth grade), s/he will take the PSAT examination as a "practice test." In his/her junior year (eleventh grade), s/he will take this exam to qualify for the National Merit Scholarship, as well as the National Hispanic Recognition Program. These exams are generally scheduled on the third Saturday in October.

As stated, the PSAT/NMSQT exam is typically administered each year on the third Saturday in October. To determine when your high school will administer this exam, go to the collegeboard.org website. To register, you must contact your counseling office, registrar, or book-keeper. The College Board does not register students for this exam, nor do they administer this exam. Registration is only done through your local high school.

Obtain PSAT results and carefully review your student's score to de-termine where improvement is needed. Then, develop a strategy to pre-pare for the actual SAT exam.

The PSAT/NMSQT examination is essential for Latino students be-cause several universities offer a full scholarship for National Hispanic Scholars. If your child scores well on this exam and has a high GPA, s/he may be given the distinction of "National Hispanic Scholar."

National Hispanic Scholar – Every school year, the National Hispanic Recognition Program (NHRP) identifies approximately 5,000 of the highest-scoring students in the U.S. who take the PSAT/NMSQT and self-identify as Hispanic/Latino. Nationwide, there are more than 200,000 juniors considered. A student who earns this distinction is re-ferred to as a "National Hispanic Scholar." Qualifying criteria for the National Hispanic Recognition Program (NHRP) varies year-to-year and by state; criteria can be found on the College Board website: www.collegeboard.org.

Subscribing universities will purchase the annual list of students who meet the National Hispanic Scholar criteria. Therefore, it is important your student check the box on their PSAT form that asks if his/her email and personal information can be shared with subscribing colleges and universities. Shortly after the scores are published, if your child meets the criteria, s/he will begin receiving recruitment letters from universities.

There are many competitive universities that offer full scholarships, housing, meals, or a stipend for a National Hispanic Scholar. Visit the financial aid page of the college(s) you are considering to determine whether they offer this scholarship. Many of these schools will waive their college application fees and essay requirement. In addition to full tuition, some of these universities offer annual stipends, a free laptop, and other perks.

SAT and ACT Exams – Students may elect to take either the ACT or the SAT. Or, they may elect to take both. Interestingly, for the last several years, more Latino students took the ACT versus the SAT. Ideally, the ACT or SAT should be taken by spring or summer of the junior year so that your student has ample time to focus on college applications in late summer and early fall of the senior year.

The ACT stands for American College Testing and tests students in English, mathematics, reading, and science, with an optional essay. Students can take this examination in lieu of the SAT. The scale of scores ranges from 1 to 36.

SAT stands for the Scholastic Aptitude Test. The SAT exam is administered by the College Board and tests students in reading, writing, and math, with an optional essay. The new version of the SAT rolled out in March 2016 with a scale of 400 points to a maximum of 1600 points.

What About Test Prep Programs? – Let me start out by saying I highly recommend Latino students take a formal test prep program. I recommend these programs because I know they work. My own children participated in prep programs, and I recommend all of the students I coach to participate in test prep programs.

How do you know which test prep program to enroll? It can be confusing because there are many, many options. There are ACT and SAT tutors, online aids, summer camps, books, tutoring centers, and preparation programs offered by a myriad of companies and individuals. So, which program should your student enroll?

In general, I recommend a classroom-based setting (versus a textbook or online help) that offers live instruction and practice tests and coincides with the timing of your student's test date. The program should focus on test-taking strategies, not subject-matter content. These types of programs are very expensive (perhaps $1,000). However, some programs offer financial aid to students. Additionally, by pooling together a group of students, you can contact the test prep company and ask for a group discount! I know several parents (myself included) who have negotiated a better rate for their group of students.

If a formal test prep program is not reasonably within your budget, then I would recommend obtaining a copy of the most recent ACT or SAT test prep book from your local library. Your student should take timed practice exams, to get into practice and become familiar with the process.

How many times should your student take the ACT or SAT? This is probably the most frequently asked question I receive from students and their parents. Obviously, they should take either the PreACT and/ or the PSAT. After this, I recommend a student do not take the ACT or SAT more than twice. After taking their first attempt, the student should carefully examine their strengths and weaknesses. Next, the student should enroll in a preparatory course. Preferably, an in-class, six to eight week course. This way, the student will be fully prepared to take their second exam with ideal results.

Let me repeat my test taking recommendation. Always take the PreACT or PSAT for a practice run. Then take the actual ACT or SAT once and carefully analyze results. Next, enroll in an in-class prep program to strategize a composite score increase. Don't take the exam more than twice. Even the College Board – the organization that designs and administers the SAT, does not recommend taking the SAT more than twice. Here's what they say:

We don't recommend taking it more than twice
because there's no evidence
that taking the SAT multiple times significantly changes your score.

Regardless of my test taking recommendation, many students will still retake their SAT or ACT multiple times without an intervention. This is a crazy strategy! Why?

Consider the quote by Albert Einstein: "Insanity: Doing the same thing over and over again and expecting different results." By taking the SAT exam over and over, without implementing a formalized preparation strategy, how will this change the outcome for your student?

Yes, through repeated attempts, your student will eventually become more familiar with the test format, structure, and timing of the exam (which is a plus). However, your student will not have learned the strategy of *how* to take the test. Moreover, the benefit of a very slight increase in the overall score will be significantly outweighed by the negative result of factors students overlook. Which factors?

Factor 1: Colleges may see all scores. Students may send their top SAT scores to universities through the process called Score Choice™.

It is an option provided by the College Board that allows students to select their best scores and send only those scores to colleges. However, highly competitive universities typically have access to *all* of students' scores, making this option a moot point. So, unless your student is confident s/he will significantly raise the score, why risk multiple repeat scores? Worse yet, what if the subsequent scores are lower than the first exam?

Additionally, many schools do not allow you to "mix and match"— meaning you cannot send different test scores from different test dates. For example, the ACT does not combine test scores from different dates. They will only release the record for the test date selected by the student.

Factor 2: Multiple exams indicate true ability. Let's say Veronica took the SAT three consecutive times, and the end result was a cumulative increase of only 20 points. This informs the Admissions officer that the final score is truly indicative of Veronica's abilities. It is reasonable to conclude Veronica could not do better than this, since three test times is a fair and reasonable assessment of her abilities. If Veronica took the exam only once, the Admissions officer might give her the benefit of the doubt that on that particular day Veronica was not performing at her optimum capacity.

Recap! Your student should take their PreACT or PSAT in October of the sophomore and junior year of high school. Then, your student should register to take the ACT or SAT in late spring or early summer of the end of the junior year. Results should be carefully analyzed for strengths and weaknesses. Next, your student should enroll in an ACT or SAT test prep program. The second ACT or SAT exam date should be scheduled to immediately coincide with the conclusion of the prep program. Finally, your student should not take the ACT or SAT more than twice.

SAT Subject Tests — In addition to the SAT or ACT examination, competitive colleges will also consider your student's SAT Subject Test scores. An SAT Subject Test is a one-hour, multiple choice examination, given in a specific subject area. There are 20 SAT Subject Tests in five subject areas, including English, languages, history, mathematics, and science. The exams are offered certain times each year, and students can take up to three tests in one sitting. The schedule and registration can be found on www.collegeboard.org. Fee waivers may be available.

Colleges consider SAT Subject Test scores for admission, and some colleges specify the subject type you must take for admission consideration (or for program-specific criteria). To determine which tests are required, visit the websites for colleges in which your student is interested. As a rule, students should take Subject Tests related to their intended major.

A tip! SAT Subject Tests can be taken individually and are offered frequently throughout the school year. Therefore, take SAT Subject Tests *immediately* following the respective high school subject matter. Many students do not understand the importance of taking these examinations when the subject matter is fresh in their mind. Waiting until the fall of their senior year and trying to take as many Subject Matter examinations as possible is not a smart strategy.

AP and IB Examinations – Advanced Placement (AP) examinations and International Baccalaureate (IB) examinations are important components for college admissions consideration. AP and IB courses are rigorous and challenging high school courses, and are considered equivalent to first-year (introductory) college level curricula. Selective colleges expect that high school students will have taken AP or IB courses available to them, along with corresponding examinations. Upon completing an AP or IB course(s), generally in grades 10—12, students will take a rigorous examination.

AP examinations are administered by the College Board each May, while IB examinations are administered through the International Baccalaureate Organization each May and November. Students who achieve a minimum score, as defined and determined by the college, may be permitted to skip the corresponding course as a freshman in college. There are currently 35 AP exams and the current fee for one AP examination is $92.00. However, the College Board provides a $29 fee reduction for low-income students.

Because most high schools in the U.S. do not offer an IB program, we are going to focus on strategies regarding the AP exams. Below is a snapshot of three important points regarding AP exams.

First point: A student does not need to complete an AP course in order to register/take the exam. Students may attend a charter school that doesn't offer AP courses for their students. Or, they may be home schooled. Or, they simply do not wish to take the coursework in order to take the exam. Some kids are just that brilliant, seriously (I've met them!). However, these students are pretty rare. If your student's high school does not offer a particular AP course, your student can take the course through an online provider such as Scout: www.ucscout.org.

Second point: Students may take an AP exam at any time during their high school career. However, in order for an AP Exam score(s) to be listed on a student's college application (in their senior year), the student must have completed the exams on or before May of their junior year. Key language: "*listed on a student's college application*." Since the exams are only administered each May, if they haven't taken an exam(s) by their junior year, they will not have exam scores to list on their fall college applications. In addition to taking AP exams for competitiveness, students will also want to strategize AP exams in order to bypass significant coursework as a freshman at their future college. #lowertuitionfees #savemoney

Third point: Let's talk about how many AP courses and exams students are taking for admission to selective colleges. To better understand how AP exam scores are evaluated by selective colleges, let's put this into context. I'm pasting below recent stats for UCLA's admitted class:

UCLA ADMITTED FRESHMAN CLASS

# of Semesters	Admit Rate	% of All Admits
Above 19	37.62%	59.28%
16-19	19.74%	18.04%

You can see that more than 75% of *admitted students* took anywhere between 16 to more than 19 semesters of Honors or AP courses. With 2 semesters equaling one year, these students took approximately 8-10 AP, IB, or honors courses. This graph is also a strong representation of what other highly competitive schools will seek.

My own kids took 10 AP courses. The students I coach typically take 8 to 10 AP courses and are gaining admission to the most selective colleges. See also, Chapter 12, "*Course Selection*." Bonus: Students may also receive recognition from the College Board ("AP Scholar Awards") by taking a certain # of exams with a qualifying score.

Certainly, there are many strategies your student can implement regarding AP or IB examinations. The key point is to know which programs exist and how to strategize the timing and selection of the accompanying coursework.

CHAPTER 15

LETTERS OF RECOMMENDATION

WHAT IS THE Letter of Recommendation? The Letter of Recommendation (LOR) is part of the college application required by some, but not all, colleges.

The letter serves as an endorsement – providing details or information not disclosed elsewhere in the application. Think of the LOR as an endorsement from a credible source. In a nutshell, it's like saying, *"I personally recommend Guadalupe. I think she would be a great addition to your campus."*

While the student's application contains statistical data (GPA, test scores, etc.) and a Personal Statement written from the student's perspective, the LOR is a secondary source that reflects a third party's view of the student's abilities, personality disposition, and other characteristics. For this reason, admissions staff glean additional information from the LOR that may not be apparent within the candidate's applicant materials.

While the LOR is an important part of the college application, high school students typically perceive the LOR as a task item – just a formality to comply with an application requirement. Trivializing the significance of the LOR can be a gamble. Many times, all things being equal, the LOR can boost the overall candidate ranking for college admission or scholarship consideration. A strong LOR may shift the perspective of the Admissions Counselor or Scholarship Committee in favor of the candidate.

Who Writes the LOR? For the Common Application the LOR will be written by two teachers and one secondary counselor. Since high school guidance counselors are generally assigned according to the last name of the student, students do not typically have leverage in selecting which counselor will write their LOR. However, students can select which of the two teachers will write their letters.

Quetzal Mama recommends students *carefully* select two strategic teachers to write their letters. Ideally, the two teachers will be those that taught the student in the junior year of high school. This is important for two reasons. First, the letter will be the most *recent* assessment by teaching staff. Remember, a LOR written by teaching staff in the senior year will only reflect approximately three months of observation and assessment. Second, the junior year teaching staff tends to be more rigorous and reflective of AP or IB level coursework (versus the freshman or sophomore years).

Keep in mind, some teachers have a policy to write only a set number of letters each school year. They typically operate on a "first-come, first-served" basis. For this reason, check with teachers *before* the end of the junior year of high school to get on the teacher's roster before summer break.

Avoid Common Mistakes in the LOR. Every year I observe the same problematic patterns with LORs. The problem I see is that the letters are misaligned with the information colleges are *really* looking for. The issue is not with the Secondary Counselors, but with the Teachers. Counselors are fairly informed regarding the appropriate content for LOR's because of their relationships with college representatives and their knowledge of the college admission process. Whereas, high school teachers' expertise is in teaching, not crafting LORs for students!

It's not the fault of the teaching staff. The problems have more to do with the highly competitive nature of the college admissions process and the sheer volume of letters teachers are required to write. Adding to the problem is the fact that many students wait until the last minute to obtain their letters (resulting in an inferior letter). I'm sharing below three common issues that come up each year with LOR's written by teachers.

First, high school teachers are largely unfamiliar with the criteria that Admissions Counselors seek. Therefore, they tend to include information *they* feel is appropriate. Teachers are unaware of the increased competitiveness through which applicant materials are considered. Therefore, they may not give credence to the importance of crafting an exceptional LOR.

Second, teachers often compose LORs that read like a resume. The letter is obviously composed as a "fill in the blanks" template. This happens because many high school districts hand out a "brag sheet" for the student to complete and give to their recommenders. This sounds efficient, but "filling in the blanks" is not an ideal strategy to obtain a winning letter.

Lastly – and I believe most importantly – the LOR content is the result of the recommender's recollection. Remember, most public high school teachers have 32 to 35 students per class, six classes per day, 10 months per year. It is difficult for many teachers to recall unique or specific details about every student. This factor is problematic because this is precisely what the admission folks want – the details!

So, what can a student do to avoid these problems? Quetzal Mama's got your back! Follow Quetzal Mama's six (6) tips for an impressive LOR.

Tip #1 – Target the Right Evaluator. The instruction to students on the Common Application regarding appropriate recommenders reads as follows: ". . . *a teacher who has taught you an academic subject.*" As stated above, I recommend students identify a teacher from their junior year of high school. Additionally, I recommend students obtain one LOR from an AP or IB teacher in the discipline they are pursuing as an undergraduate.

For example, if Blanca intends to major in Computer Science, then she will want at least one letter from her Honors Pre-Calculus or AP Calculus teacher (if she has taken this course). For the second teacher, Blanca may consider a non "hard science" recommender – perhaps her AP English or AP U.S. History teacher.

Tip #2 – Plan One School Year Ahead. Students will be asking two teachers for a LOR in the fall of their senior year. Students should form relationships with targeted individuals through scheduled meetings, sharing of research projects and/or term papers, or having general discussions. The point of building this relationship is to stand out in the teacher or counselor's mind by conveying intellectual curiosity, demonstrating commitment to future educational goals, and demonstrating maturity.

Tip #3 – Ask to See the Letter. Students should never accept a blind letter of recommendation! A "blind" letter is a letter submitted to the colleges that your student has not reviewed. It means your student has no idea whether the recommender is providing a positive or negative recommendation or whether the recommender is highlighting desired and important aspects of the student's academic profile.

Unless the "blind letter" rule is the published policy or practice at your student's high school, this is a huge red flag. It is too risky to submit letters where the student has no idea what is said about him or her. Although this is not a common practice, I have run across a handful of teachers in the past several years who tell the student outright they will not share the contents of their letter.

Tip #4 – Be Involved in the Process. No, this does not mean the student writes the letter! Being involved in the process refers to an agreed upon collaboration between the teacher and the student. It means the student will have asked the teacher in advance whether or not they may provide details, anecdotal references, or samples of their work.

In my experience, nearly 99% of teachers asked by students are open to an informal collaborative process. It seems that the majority of teachers welcome content suggestions from students to increase accuracy and relevancy of the LOR.

¡Cuídate! Being "involved in the process" does not mean writing the letter for the evaluator. The role of the evaluator is to assess the student's strengths *honestly*. The student's involvement should be limited to proofing, offering suggestions, recommending additions or deletions, and reviewing for tone and overall content. Since the LOR is a component of the admissions process, students must respect and adhere to the integrity of this process.

Tip #5 – Make it Easy for your Evaluator. Now that the student has found an appropriate evaluator, the student should provide the evaluator with helpful information to draft the letter. Helpful information refers to written papers, projects, and any other noteworthy examples of his or her work (including references to classroom discussions led by the student).

I recommend students go directly to the "Background Information" and "Ratings" section of the Teacher Evaluation Form on the Common Application. This can be found online at www.commonapp.org. There are 15 evaluation criteria (on a 7 rank scale) that teachers will complete on behalf of the student. Students should use these 15 questions as a guide; type up specific examples for each topic; and use these examples as a reference guide.

Tip #6 – Quantify and Qualify. Since the evaluators will already have ranked the student in the "Ratings" section, and the student would have provided detailed examples for each of the 15 rankings, the letter is practically written already! Now, the challenge is to further quantify and qualify statements within the letter. The prompt the teacher evaluators receive reads as follows:

Please write whatever you think is important about this student, including a description of academic and personal characteristics, as demonstrated in your classroom. We welcome information that will help us to differentiate this student from others.

You can see from the above instructions that the objective is for the evaluator to provide a descriptive analysis that supports the recommendation. Therefore, the letter should **not** state, "Cesar is a great student" or "Cesar is really smart." Instead, it should read something like this:

"In terms of intellectual promise, Cesar easily ranks in the top 1% of students I've taught in the last 12 years. Evidence of Cesar's intellectual ability is evident through his writing and classroom discussions. For example, Cesar led a provocative classroom discussion regarding American identity. He challenged many common beliefs and presented concise and convincing arguments one would typically see in an introductory college level course. Subsequently, Cesar expounded on this topic by presenting

a highly analytical and thought-provoking essay regarding the concept of "American exceptionalism." Compared to other student's I have taught over the years, Cesar's keen ability to grasp complex and sophisticated concepts, his exceptional critical thinking skills, maturity level, and his ability to form understanding from subtle nuances, renders my unconditional and enthusiastic endorsement as a candidate for admission to your university.

You can see that this letter quantifies Cesar's intellectual abilities; provides insight into Cesar's intellectual curiosity and critical thinking skills; and addresses his maturity level. The above example has been shortened for this chapter. However, the letter should not be less than ¾ of a page, and not more than one page.

In terms of qualifying and quantifying your student's work, here are four important factors to keep in mind:

Intellectual Abilities. The letter should qualify your student's intellectual abilities compared to other students the teacher has taught. For example, the teacher may state your student represents the top one to five percent of the class in terms of intellectual abilities. This assessment could be gleaned from exam grades and homework grades, or based on perceived ability. Perceived ability may not necessarily reflect homework, midterm grades, or other established benchmarks. It could be perceived through the student's demonstrated intellectual curiosity or potential.

Anecdotal Reference. A strong letter should include a personal, anecdotal reference. This will include reference to your student's academic ability demonstrated in a number of ways. For example, an exemplary class discussion, an outstanding report or presentation, or a well written essay. Your student's teacher will not likely remember all of these little tidbits, so it is your student's responsibility to refresh the teacher's memory by providing a written or verbal summary. Teachers have far too many students to recall at this level, so they will appreciate your student's examples.

Personal Disposition. In addition to describing your student's academic promise, the recommender should also address your student's character strengths as they relate to competitive universities. For example, if your student is disciplined and mature, the teacher should express how these strengths are beneficial in handling rigorous college curriculum. Finally, if your student is in the top of his/her class, it would not hurt for the teacher to say your student is also a humble person.

Special Circumstances. If your student has special circumstances not addressed in the application, the teacher should describe these circumstances within the letter. Special circumstances include non-academic factors that have impacted your student's ability to perform or obstacles s/he has had to overcome. For example, the teacher can emphasize spending a significant amount of time per week (e.g., 20 hours) working in a job, being the primary caregiver for a handicapped parent or sibling, or dealing with other extenuating circumstances.

Note that the letter should **not** include a listing of all of your student's classes, extracurricular activities, and awards. The Admissions officer already has this information within the application. Instead, the teacher might focus on a particular skill or talent related to the student's intended major. For example, if your student is pursuing a political science major and this teacher heads the Mock Trial Club at the school, it would be advantageous for the teacher to reference your student's talent and abilities in this particular activity. Similarly, if your student's math teacher is also the Mathematics Chair, a discussion about your student's intellectual prowess in AP Calculus would go a long way.

Rule of Thumb: The content of the letter must specify, measure, quantify, or assess your student's academic talents and intellectual abilities. Your student is a scholar, competing with other scholars. Admissions officers want to know how your student compares with others at his/her school. For more information regarding the timing and method to submit letters of recommendation in the Common Application, go to Chapter 21, "*Think You're Ready to Apply?*"

A few final suggestions! Once the impressive and well-crafted LORs are completed, students should request that they receive a generic printout of the letter to be used for future scholarships, internships, or leadership programs. The teacher or counselor letter can be dated as "Fall 2017" and addressed To Whom it May Concern (or alternately, "Scholarship Committee"). The student should print several of these letters to have on file for future applications.

Finally, students should not forget to thank the recommender. No, an email or text message will not suffice. Instead, send a hand written thank you card and enclose a $5 Starbucks card or deliver some home-made cookies. Remember, the recommender has spent a significant amount of his or her personal time. Thank them!

If you'd like to see and hear Quetzal Mama's 1.5 hour "**Letter of Recommendation for Latino Students**" workshop or webinar, send an inquiry to info@quetzalmama.com.

CHAPTER 16

EARLY ACTION VERSUS REGULAR DECISION

APPLYING TO COLLEGE has become incredibly complex. There are private universities, public colleges, and Ivy Leagues—all with unique timelines and application-filing procedures. How do you know which application-filing process is advantageous for your student? In this chapter we will discuss the differences between Early Admission and Regular Admission.

Early Action or Early Decision programs are incredibly advantageous for applicants. Your student should apply to the first choice through this early process, if the college offers this option. An "early" option is beneficial in three ways.

- Students nearly always gain a statistical edge by applying early.
- Some universities provide financial aid award incentives with their early admission notice.
- Students learn early (usually around the second week of December) whether or not they are admitted to their top choice.

Statistically, a college will generally admit approximately 25 percent of candidates who apply Early Action. It only takes a quick glance at admissions statistics from top schools to understand how this is advantageous. For highly selective colleges, Regular Decision applicants will yield about a 6 percent to 10 percent admittance rate. Compare this with 25 percent of Early Action and Early Decision rates; it is easy to see why your student should use this strategy for a first choice.

Keep in mind, one of the main reasons students have a statistical admission advantage as an *early* candidate is because the typical applicant in the early pool represents the top 5% to 10% of students across the US. These same students would have high odds of admission whether applying early admission or regular admission. In other words, your student will not have increased odds of admission simply by applying early. The admission advantage is for those students who are exceptionally well prepared *and* submit an early application. Below are the key definitions of early admission programs.

Early Action – There are two different ways to apply "Early" to a university. One way is referred to as Early Action and the other is Early Decision. Early Decision is a **binding** agreement, while Early Action is non-binding. There is also a subset of the "Early" application process called Restrictive Early Action or Single Choice Early Action, both of which are non-binding. Generally, students must submit an application on or before November 1 at midnight, to apply "Early." Some colleges have a November 15 deadline.

Applicants applying Early Action may apply to other colleges under the Regular Decision process but may not apply to any other college under either Early Action, Early Decision, or Restrictive Early Action (sometimes referred to as "Single Choice Early Action"). This means your student can apply to Stanford Restrictive Early Action, receive admission notification in early December (versus March 30 or later), and maintain applicant status at any other college where an application has been submitted. Your student does not need to accept Stanford's offer of admission and can wait until May 1 to accept a preferred offer of admission.

I recommend Early Action (or Restrictive Early Action) for the students I coach because it offers the greatest flexibility with regard to financial aid awards. Early Decision (defined below) requires the student to accept the admission offer upon early notification, thereby declining any other admission offers from one or multiple universities. This has a detrimental financial impact on Latino students because it does not allow them to consider or negotiate other financial aid awards.

Early Decision – Unlike Early Action (as defined above), Early Decision is a binding agreement. If your student is admitted via Early Decision, then s/he is required to attend that college and must withdraw all other applications. I do not see the strategic or financial advantage to applying Early Decision when your student has other "Early" options that are non-binding.

Regular Decision – Regular Decision is the traditional college application process. Students apply by the posted application deadline (generally January 1) and receive admission notification late spring (generally March 30) of their senior year of high school. An admission decision may be rendered sooner than March 30 if the campus is on a "Rolling Admission" cycle. It is a non-binding process, and students may apply to as many schools as they wish via "Regular Decision." An admission decision by the student is made on or before May 1.

The following chart illustrates the differences between the different types of applications:

Application Type	Is This Binding?	May I Apply "Early" to Other Colleges?	May I Apply "Regular Decision" to Other Colleges?
Early Decision	Yes	No	Yes*
Early Action	No	Some allow	Yes
Restrictive Early Action	No	No	Yes
Single Choice Early Action	No	No	Yes

If admitted Early Decision, student must withdraw all other applications and cannot accept any other offers of admission.

CHAPTER 17

THE PERSONAL STATEMENT

THE PERSONAL STATEMENT is Quetzal Mama's signature expertise. Fortunately, there are several ways students can "nail" their Personal Statement with help from Quetzal Mama.

First, students may attend a Quetzal Mama Personal Statement Bootcamp in their State. The boot camps are held throughout the U.S. These camps are limited to 20 students per boot camp. See www.quetzalmama.com for more information. Want to bring Quetzal Mama to your state? Contact us!

Second, if students are unable to attend an in-person Boot Camp, they may receive Quetzal mama coaching *virtually*—via an online webinar. To reserve your student's spot at the next personal statement webinar, see the schedule at www.quetzalmama.com. Quetzal Mama personal statement webinars typically run July through November each year.

Third, for students unable to attend an in-person boot camp or virtual webinar, they can still receive Quetzal Mama's comprehensive tools, methods, and culturally-relevant strategies in the latest book, *"Nailed It! Quetzal Mama's Toolkit for Extraordinary College Essays."* The book provides students with first-hand examples of how to pick the right prompt, how to effectively market their profile, how best to articulate unique qualities, and how to avoid some common mistakes. If your high school counseling center or local public library does not yet have this book in stock, ask them to order it.

Lastly, if students cannot attend a boot camp or webinar and unable to get a copy of the book *"Nailed It!"* I'm sharing a brief overview of the personal statement process below.

What is the Personal Statement?

The Personal Statement is an essay required by most selective colleges and universities. There are generally three types of college applications that require an essay or Personal Statement, including:

1. Private Colleges – typically utilizing the Common Application;
2. Public Research Universities including "Research 1" universities – utilizing their proprietary application for all campuses within their region or state; and
3. Private Universities that do not use the Common Application.

Private Colleges – The Common Application is an online application used by more than 500 private universities and colleges in the US. A student completes one "common" application that can be sent to multiple universities. Currently the Common App requires one 650-word Personal Statement (and some campuses require additional supplemental essays).

Public Research Universities – These include, but are not limited, to institutions such as University of California, University of Texas, or University of Colorado. These campuses have their own application and essay requirements.

Private Universities that do not use the Common Application – Finally, there are selective universities that use neither of the above and instead have their own application and essays. Some of these campuses include Georgetown, MIT, and Rutgers, to name a few.

How is the Essay Used in College Admissions?

The essay provides an opportunity for the student to articulate to the admissions team why s/he is a unique candidate. It gets the admission reader beyond stats – GPA, class rank, ACT or SAT score. It allows the reader to know the student personally, providing a glimpse into unique life experiences, such as:

- Passion for a particular discipline (Biological Sciences, Journalism, Engineering, etc.);
- Factors that influenced academic performance respective to the high school campus;
- An appreciation for the student's cultural authenticity/ diversity;
- Obstacles the student overcame along the academic journey;
- All of the special details that help admissions folks learn the unique characteristics and attributes – the particular skills, strengths, and disposition that separate one candidate from others.

In addition to reflecting on how a student's essay will be used, we need to talk about the application. Admissions teams will be evaluating your student's application on three dimensions.

First, admission officers will assess academic accomplishments. This can be easily discerned by the student's transcript and statistical data listed on the application. This includes GPA, class rank, and performance on standardized college exams such as the SAT/ACT, SAT Subject Tests, and AP or IB Exam scores.

Second, admission officers will review extracurricular activities. This will also be discerned through the application via various on-campus clubs, sports, and leadership activities, as well as outside volunteer and community service activities.

Lastly, admission officers will consider personal qualities and character. This factor is a little tricky because qualities and character cannot be objectively discerned through a list of activities or statistical analysis.

For this reason, selective universities use a "holistic" approach or "comprehensive review" in screening applicants. This means the *entire* student profile will be considered – both the unique background and academic statistics.

While the admissions reader may assume certain qualities and characteristics by reviewing an application, the best way for a student to tell their story (and take advantage of the holistic review process) is through the Personal Statement. Admission teams carefully screen the statement to determine whether or not the student will be a complimentary addition to their entering freshman class.

Who Reads It?

In addition to the Admissions staff, additional readers will likely include faculty within the proposed discipline; college admission consultants; alumni; and in some cases, contracted essay readers unaffiliated with the university. These experienced essay readers will plow through each essay, evaluating and scoring *in three minutes or less*. During the admissions cycle, readers will read essays all day, for months at a time.

How is this Statement Unique to Latino Students?

Based on my experience, culturally authentic Latino students and/or first generation, low-income, historically underrepresented students have an edge when it comes to writing the Personal Statement.

No, this doesn't mean "minority" students are assessed with "special" criteria (aka lower academic standards) than their non-minority peers. *This is a myth.* Let's be clear. Selective colleges have a general academic benchmark that students must meet to be considered for admission, period. However, once students have met that benchmark, they have an opportunity to shine within their Personal Statement.

So, what type of edge do Latino students have? We have an edge in the common themes we often write about. For example, our stories are often central to our cultural identity. When we consider that highly selective colleges typically admit only 10 to 20% Latino students, this means the diversity we write about has value in this context. We can share how our unique life experiences will contribute to a diversified student body.

Additionally, our stories often represent the personal qualities of grit, determination, resilience, and as we say, *ganas*. These traits are especially appealing in a Personal Statement. Only those students who have authentically experienced challenges and obstacles can articulate these qualities in their essay.

Now, I'm not saying that all Latino students must write about overcoming adversity, or focus exclusively on cultural authenticity. Truthfully, there are millions of ways a Latino student can approach the Personal Statement. The key is to articulate the most compelling story that best highlights the overall profile of the student candidate.

JUST TELL ME THE BOTTOM LINE!

The bottom line is that Personal Statement is a critical component of the college application. It helps admission officers learn more about the student – aside from academic stats. The Statement should be written in the summer, and not late in Fall. See Chapter 20, "*High School Timelines at a Glance*" for more information on deadlines. If applying Early Action, the Personal Statement will accompany the application due on November 1. If Regular Admission, the Statement will accompany the application due January 1.

If your students would like to craft an exceptional personal statement for college admissions, get your copy of Quetzal Mama's Toolkit for Extraordinary College Essays on Amazon or Barnes & Noble:

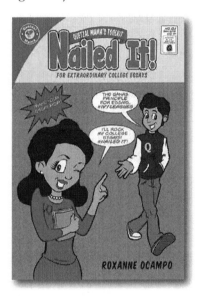

CHAPTER 18

HOW TO SELECT THE RIGHT COLLEGE

I'M SHARING THIS chapter because I want your student to utilize a sound college selection strategy to increase their odds of admission. This is especially important for low-income students. Why? Because low-income students are eligible to receive Fee Waivers for their applications. Students who do not use waivers wisely may "waste" all of them by applying to colleges misaligned with their academic profile. This chapter will help your student avoid this tragic outcome!

Using fee waivers wisely means avoiding the phenomenon called, *Overmatching*. This should not to be confused with the phenomenon of *Undermatching*:

> *Overmatching* occurs when mid-level college ready students apply for admission to selective colleges where they are underqualified.

> *Undermatching* refers to high-performing, college ready students who select and enroll in colleges with selectivity levels significantly lower than their academic profile or forego applying to college altogether.

Although some college "experts" use convoluted formulas to calculate acceptance odds based on GPA, rank, SAT scores, strength of curriculum, etc., an absolute theory to predetermine chances of admission does not exist. For this reason, I created a common sense tool to pick the *right* college, called the "*80-10-10 Rule.*" From my years of working with students, I have found this to be the simplest and most effective, common sense tool to determine a student's reasonable chance of admission.

The 80-10-10 Rule – The 80-10-10 rule means that 80% of colleges applied should be "match" campuses; 10% should be "reach" campuses and 10% should be "safety" campuses. Following Quetzal Mama's rule of 20 colleges, that means 16 will be "matches," two will be "reaches," and two will be "safeties." To implement the 80-10-10 Rule, follow these three steps.

First, the student will identify his/her academic profile. The profile consists of the SAT or ACT scores, GPA and class rank, and scores from SAT Subject Tests and AP or IB exam scores.

Second, the student reviews the *admitted* (not 'applicants') freshman profile for the colleges being considered. To do this, the student will visit the website for the colleges they are interested in applying. Nearly all competitive colleges will have a profile of entering freshman listed on their Admissions web page.

Lastly, the student will compare his/her profile with the profile of students being admitted. Your student will know immediately whether their profile is consistent with the profile of students admitted to the college. That's it! You don't need a calculator or a sophisticated algorithm. There is nothing mysterious about this formula if you use this common sense approach.

Alternatively, your student may use an online tool to find colleges aligned with their profile. While there are many such websites available, be careful! Some of these sites are marketing machines geared toward collecting student profiles in order to promote their products and services. My students tell me the "Big Future" website hosted by the College Board is a very helpful tool using the filter "*Test Scores and Selectivity*" found at bigfuture.collegeboard.org.

Now that your student has his/her academic stats available, and a list of contenders, it's time to place the colleges into three different bins. These will represent "match," "reach," and "safety" campuses.

Match School – A "Match" campus is one in which your student's scores are closely aligned or "match" the admitted student profile of the entering freshman class. Some experts recommend that scores are within 5% of admitted student profile scores.

For example, let's consider Stanford University. Currently, the admit rate is around 5% to 6%. Typically, admitted students to Stanford have composite SAT scores between 2070 and 2350, with an average GPA around 3.9. Likewise, the typical admitted student holds an average ACT composite score of 32. This data should provide students with a general idea of whether or not they are a match for this campus. With a 5% to 6% admit rate, you can easily see that most students will not be admitted.

Using the Stanford example, if Marisol has a composite SAT of 2100 and a 3.95 GPA, then Stanford is a "match" campus for her. Conversely, if Marisol has a 1600 SAT composite score and a 3.4 GPA this would not be a "match" campus. However, putting this in context, ultra-competitive schools like Stanford are nearly always considered a "reach" campus for nearly all students simply because of the very small number of admits each year.

Reach School – The Ivies and most of the ultra-selective private universities should be considered "reach" campuses for most students. This is simply due to numbers – where upwards of 90% of students are denied admission each year. Aside from this ultra-selective group, a reach school is defined as a campus where the student's academic profile is moderately below the average profile of admitted students. The emphasis should be on "*moderately below*" the average and not significantly or extremely outside of the range of acceptable scores. In other words, a reach campus should not be confused with a "dream" school (based on fantasy, not reality) where the odds of admission are extremely low.

Safety School –A Safety School is a college where your student will most likely receive admission because his/her profile is *superior* to the average profile of students admitted.

For example, we will look at Miguel who has an un-weighted GPA of 4.0, a composite SAT score of 2080, and a ranking of No. 2 in his class. Miguel would not consider Yale or Princeton "Safety Schools" because he cannot be certain he will receive admission to their campuses. And, his overall academic scores would not be considered superior to the typical admitted student. Plus – I'll say it again – no student should consider any Ivy League campus as a "safety" school due to the incredibly selective and competitive criteria. For Miguel, his safety campuses would include less selective universities where his scores are *superior* to the average profile.

Note! Students should only apply to safety campuses that are truly viable options for enrollment. In other words, a student should never apply to safety campuses when they have no intention (or desire) to attend that school. Safety campuses should be selected with the same thought, analysis, and time as the match campuses. In the extremely rare instance a student is denied to all of their matched campuses, they must be prepared to attend a safety campus. This can be devastating for students who did not put thought or effort into selecting safety campuses.

An exception! There are some exceptional instances where a student may indeed receive admission to a college although his/her academic profile is significantly below the average range of admitted students. However, in these uncommon instances the student generally has compelling attributes or talents, extenuating circumstances, or some other unknown factor that mitigated test scores or GPA's. For this reason, I always encourage students to apply to their "dream school," but use the remainder of applications for campuses more closely aligned with their academic profiles.

Quetzal Mama Recommends 20 Campuses – I recommend students apply to 20 campuses for two important reasons.

First, based on sheer numbers, applying to 20 campuses using the 80-10-10 rule means the student will yield the greatest odds of admission. Having more offers of admission means the student has greater odds of receiving superior financial aid packages. Applying to only three or four campuses is limiting when you consider the numerical odds.

The second reason is because qualifying (income-eligible) students receive fee waivers for their *private* college applications. Therefore, there is no reason to limit the number of campuses to only a few. How does this work?

If your student received a fee waiver for their PSAT or SAT, they will be eligible for a fee waiver used for their college applications. For my students in California, they receive 4 fee waivers to the California State University system and 4 fee waivers for the University of California system. That's 8 waivers. Then, they will apply to 12 private colleges using the Common Application and applying fee waivers to these campuses. That means these students will not pay any out of pocket expenses for their 20 college applications.

Lastly, applying to 20 campuses allows the student to apply to a broad mix of in-state, out-of-state, public and private campuses, spanning diverse geographic regions. Because financial aid packages vary greatly from campus-to-campus (and even within the same college system), a student's odds of receiving a strong package increases by casting a wider net.

Recap! In a nutshell, income-eligible students should apply to 20 campuses using the *80-10-10 Rule*. They should know their academic profile and select a total of 20 campuses with 80% matches, 10% reaches, and 10% safety campuses. In addition to selecting campuses that match their academic profile, there are other factors a student should consider when selecting their list of 20 colleges. Some of these factors include:

Curriculum for your Major
Geographic Preference
Public or Private
Campus Size
Internship & Research Opportunities
Leverage for Graduate School
On-Campus Organizations
Diversity & Inclusion
Financial Aid Programs
Graduation Rates

CHAPTER 19

THE COLLEGE INTERVIEW

MOST, BUT NOT all competitive universities invite students to interview. The interview can be on campus (if you have scheduled a trip), can be held at your high school campus (where a representative visits your site), or it can be at a designated location coordinated by their alumni association.

What the Interview Is and Is Not —The interview is not a make-or-break meeting. It is only a point of reference for the university. The meeting can either confirm what the university already knows about your student, or it may (in rare cases) provide the university with a unique perspective they did not obtain through the application.

The interview may also be a means to gauge the college's potential yield. If a student declines an interview from a particular college, this may be viewed as an indication the college is not the top choice of the applicant. If the college offers admission and the student declines, this impacts their "yield." A yield is the percentage of admitted students who accept the admission offer and matriculate (or enroll) in their college.

Two important facts about interviews. First, an interview is not necessarily an indication of a student's candidacy for admission. For example, many selective colleges offer an interview to *every student* who applies. Second, not all colleges offer interviews. Some only offer to students who live in regions where they have alumni interviewers available, and others do not offer interviews at all.

So what happens during the interview? Generally, the interviews are very informal. The interviewer will usually be an alumnus of the college and request to meet in a public space like Starbucks. The interview may also be at a local business. In our region, the MIT interviews took place at the alumni member's personal residence in a gated foothill community.

Interview Tips —So as not to give away any college interview secrets, I will only provide the general, consistent topics that arise in most of my student's interviews.

Colleges generally want to know why the student has applied to their campus, his/her general interests, and any background information.

Most of the time, the interview will be an informal discussion. Sometimes the interviewer will do almost all of the talking (more of a recruitment attempt versus a bona fide interview), and sometimes the interviewer will ask very open-ended questions.

To prepare for the interview, the student should do two things. First, the student should consider the following commonly asked questions:

- Why did you apply to our university?
- What key programs or resources attracted you to our campus?
- Tell me about your favorite extracurricular activities.
- What is your favorite subject in high school and why?
- Tell me about a book you have recently read that was not assigned in class.
- Describe any obstacles you have encountered and how you responded.

Second, the student may wish to research the interviewer. This includes searching for the interviewer's name and biography on the

Internet. The biography will likely include the interviewer's educational background and academic interests, as well as the names of organizations in which the interviewer is involved and/or board appointments. Knowing the academic and political influences of this interviewer may come in handy when formulating answers to interview questions.

For example, when my daughter interviewed with Princeton, she conducted a thorough online search of her interviewer. She was fortunate her interviewer was a scientist and, therefore, had published research papers online. She also found his curriculum vitae (CV) online and noted his strong interest in physics. A week before her interview, she spent time studying physics; specifically, String Theory. During their conversation, Gabi introduced String Theory and they had a lengthy and lively discussion. Incidentally, she received a very compelling financial aid package from Princeton!

If you'd like detailed tips on how to nail the college interview – everything from what to wear, what to say, and what to bring – see the blog post, "I'm Scared: I have a College Interview!" on the Quetzal Mama website: www.quetzalmama.com.

CHAPTER 20

HIGH SCHOOL TIMELINES AT A GLANCE

THERE ARE MANY important college application due dates that all occur within a short period of time. The following timelines are listed in the order your student should process them. Descriptions of these items are detailed in the previous chapters as well as the *Glossary*. For parents interested in timelines for K-5 and middle school students, they are contained in Chapter 8, "*Set Up a Game Plan.*"

FRESHMAN YEAR OF HIGH SCHOOL

- Earn the highest grades possible.
- Take honors courses, if available.
- Enroll in rigorous courses aligned with target colleges/major.
- Follow the "Big Four" strategy outlined in Chapter 8, "*Set Up a Game Plan.*"
- Develop a 12-month plan to prepare for the PSAT.
- Join on-campus club(s).
- Get involved in community service (100 hours).
- Find a summer internship.
- Begin building student resume.
- Read a TON of books.

Sophomore Year of High School

- Earn the highest grades possible.
- Take Pre-AP, Pre-IB, or Honors course, if available.
- Enroll in rigorous courses aligned with target colleges/major.
- Register for and take the PSAT (third Saturday in October).
- Prepare and register for SAT Subject-Matter tests (obtain fee waivers, if possible).
- Complete 100 hours of community service.
- Begin building a cyber profile.
- Update the resume.
- Find a summer internship.
- Read a TON of books.
- Start saving money for an ACT or SAT Preparation Course.
- Start saving money for college application fees (if unqualified for fee waivers)

Junior Year of High School

- Earn the highest grades possible.
- Take Advanced Placement, IB, or Honors courses available.
- Early fall, identify and apply to summer programs with early application deadlines.
- Early fall, identify and apply to any potential "Fly-In" Programs.
- Complete 100 hours of community service.
- Continue building a cyber profile.
- Create a list of scholarships by deadline dates.
- Register and take the PSAT (third Saturday in October) to qualify for the National Hispanic Scholar and/or National Merit Scholarship.
- Register and take SAT or ACT examination (winter or spring).

- Plan and register for SAT Subject-Matter tests.
- Plan and register for AP and IB exams (exams are in May)
- Visit colleges during spring break and summer to narrow your school choices.
- Take summer courses from a local community college or university.
- Update your resume.
- Identify and apply to summer internship opportunities.
- Read a TON of books.

SENIOR YEAR OF HIGH SCHOOL

- Earn the highest grades possible.
- Finalize 20 campuses to apply (See *80-10-10 Rule*, Chapter 18)
- Obtain letters of recommendation from two teachers and one guidance counselor during first month of school.
- Complete draft versions of the Personal Statement and Supplemental Essays by September 1.
- Final opportunity to take SAT or ACT examination completed by October, if applying Early Action (November deadline).
- Final opportunity to take SAT or ACT examination completed by November or December, if applying Regular Decision.
- Update resume to include extracurricular, academic distinction, awards, honors, etc.
- Register online for the Common Application in mid to late August.
- Register for private and public universities that do not subscribe to the Common Application.
- Send official test scores to selected colleges.
- Final clean-up of cyber profile.
- Create "cheat sheet" for college applications and interviews by mid-December.

- Apply to national college match and scholarship opportunities including QuestBridge (due September) and Gates Millennium Scholars Program (due January)
- Apply for scholarships (most scholarships have a January through April 1st deadline).

You can see that beginning as early as the freshmen year I have recommended students take Advanced Placement, IB, or Honors courses, if available. Many students will not take these courses until their junior year. However, refer to Chapter 8, "*Set Up a Game Plan*," and view the acceleration strategy for higher level curriculum.

Important Financial Aid "Task Items" for Parents – In addition to student timelines, here are two important tasks parents should calendar:

- Winter of your student's senior year of high school: Compile prior year's IRS tax documents to complete FAFSA by the priority deadline. Filing of the FAFSA is due prior to March 2 of your student's senior year of high school.
- If your student intends to apply to private colleges that require the "CSS Profile," in addition to the FAFSA you will need the prior year's tax return information. Gather these documents in October of your student's senior year of high school. See "CSS Profile" in *Glossary*.

An important note about financial aid: Federal and state financial aid are allocated to those who qualify *and* timely submit their FAFSA. This is a critical deadline for parents. If your student qualifies for financial aid, but the federal monies are depleted because you submitted the FAFSA after the priority deadline, your student may not receive the financial aid to which s/he is entitled. Visit www.fafsa.ed.gov.

Why Read a TON of Books? – Every year I have emphasized, "Read a TON of books." This is an important, annual component for students for many reasons. Voracious readers perform exceptionally well in the critical reading portion of the SAT and on the writing portion of the ACT; Reading and writing go hand-in-hand. This level of reading will assist students in writing essays throughout their high school career, during the critical essay portion of the college application, and while writing scholarship essays.

Additionally, on the college application – several universities ask students to list literature that was "recently" read outside of their required school reading list. Additionally, during the interview the recruiter may say, "Tell me about a book that has influenced the way you think?"

Students should supplement their reading with additional works read during breaks and summer months. Ideally, your student's reading list will include thought-provoking works (Latino philosophers would be ideal) as well as topics aligned with your student's intended college major.

CHAPTER 21

THINK YOU'RE READY TO APPLY?

MANY STUDENTS ARE caught off guard when it comes time to prepare and submit their college applications. There are so many components to the application, along with deadlines and planning, that it can seem intimidating and overwhelming.

To streamline this process, let's glance through the following items to ensure your student is on track. If your student is truly ready to apply to college, s/he should already have completed the following by Fall of the senior year:

- Received Official Scores for the SAT or ACT exam, Subject Matter tests, and AP and IB Examinations
- Implemented *80-10-10 Rule* (identifying Match, Reach, and Safeties)
- Narrowed List of 20 Colleges
- Selected Colleges Offering Academic Major
- Strategized Geographic Diversity
- Determined Early Action or Regular Decision
- Designed a Resume Aligned with Applications
- Created a "Cheat Sheet" for Colleges Applying
- Reviewed and Obtained Letters of Recommendation
- Finalized the Personal Statement and Supplemental Essays
- Applied for Fee Waivers (or set aside funds for application fees)

Received Official Scores – See Chapter 14, "*College Entrance Exams*" to ensure the student has taken the *right* types of exams for the intended major and for the selectivity of the campus. Additionally, students should carefully review the admissions page for the narrowed colleges they wish to apply to ensure official scores are sent prior to the application deadlines for Early or Regular admission.

Implemented the 80-10-10 Rule – See Chapter 18, "*How to Select the Right College.*" In a nutshell, your student should have narrowed their "shortlist" of 20 campuses that reflect 80% match; 10% reach; and 10% safety campuses. This shortlist should be carefully aligned with your student's academic profile to yield the greatest odds of admission.

Selected Colleges Offering Academic Major – Your child will not be the first student to become enamored by the name and prestige of a college. In doing so, students overlook the reason they are pursuing higher education in the first place: to receive an education in a designated field of study. Bottom line: if the college does not offer your student's major, it is not a sound strategy.

Strategized Geographic Diversity – Geographic diversity is an important factor when selecting which 20 colleges to apply. Because Latinos tend to stick to schools close to home, it's important to know how geographic diversity may impact college admission odds (See Chapter 11, *Ave Enjaulado*). Most selective colleges hope to attract students from all over the U.S. Their belief is that their academic community benefits from a diversified pool of students representing geographically diverse backgrounds. However, just because your student is from a rural or "geographically diverse" area doesn't automatically give him/her an advantage in the admissions process.

Narrowed List of 20 Universities – Now that your student has included campuses based on geographic diversity as well as those that offer the academic major, s/he is ready to begin compiling the list of 20 campuses to submit applications. If the student follows the 80-10-10 Rule this means 80% of campuses will be "matches," 10% of campuses will be "reaches," and 10% of campuses will be "safeties." If the student is utilizing Fee Waivers, that means four waivers for state colleges, four waivers for second tier state colleges, and 12 waivers for private colleges using the Common Application. See Chapter 18, *"How to Select the Right College."*

Determined Early Action versus Regular Decision – After reading Chapter 16, *"Early Action Versus Regular Decision,"* it's time to decide which of these options is the superior strategy. If selecting an early option, ensure your student understands the process and has selected the campus which will yield the greatest odds of admission.

Designed a Resume Aligned with Applications – One of the smartest things your student can do ahead of time is to create a resume. Although a formal resume is not typically required by most colleges, it is a very smart thing to have. First, the contents of the resume can be designed to align with the actual college application. Students who take time to craft appropriate and compelling language in a resume will be able to "cut and paste" directly into the application. The content of the college application is very similar to the content of a resume – including academic honors, extracurricular activities, and work experience. Having this information already composed in a resume saves a lot of time and reduces anxiety. Second, the resume can be used as an attachment for many scholarship applications.

Created a "Cheat Sheet" – As your student is researching and compiling the list of 20 colleges, it is important that s/he maintains a "cheat sheet." This is a document that contains important information about the various colleges such as special academic programs, research programs, renowned faculty, and extracurricular activities unique to the campus. When the time comes to write the supplemental essays and/or conduct the college interview, much of the information will be contained in the careful notes the student collected.

Reviewed and Obtained Letters of Recommendation – While most private colleges require two letters of recommendation from teachers and one letter from the Secondary Counselor, many public colleges do *not* require these letters. It is your student's responsibility to monitor carefully whether the designated writers submit their forms to the Common Application prior to the application deadline. The recently improved Common Application contains automated tools to help the student keep track of which recommenders have submitted letters and which are pending. Prior to requesting a letter be uploaded for the application, the student should have carefully reviewed the contents of all letters being submitted on his/her behalf. Note that the same teacher and counselor letters will go to *all* of the colleges to which your student applies. See Chapter 15, "*Letters of Recommendation.*"

Finalized the Personal Statement and Supplemental Essays – If your student is applying to the Common Application, a 650-word essay is required that will go to all colleges applied. In addition, some selective campuses will also require supplemental essays. Furthermore, if your student is applying to campuses that do not use the Common Application – like Georgetown, MIT, or Rutgers, then a separate essay (or set of essays) is also required. Lastly, there are many public universities that have their own application and essay prompts. It is important that your student has crafted these essays far in advance. For strategies to "nail" the Personal Statement, get "*Nailed It! Quetzal Mama's Toolkit for Extraordinary College Essays.*"

Applied for Fee Waivers – Today, application fees for some private colleges can range from $75 to $90 for one application! Fortunately, income eligible students who have taken the SAT or the SAT Subject Test using a Fee Waiver will receive Fee Waivers for college applications. For example, in California qualifying students receive four (4) University of California fee waivers *and* four (4) California State University fee waivers. Typically, these fee waivers are delivered electronically by the

College Board to students in August. If your student is applying to private colleges and is income eligible, s/he may apply to any private college using the Common Application and receive a fee waiver. For this reason, I advise students to apply to a broad range of colleges because they will not pay out of pocket fees for their applications. Thank goodness for fee waivers!

CLOSING

I HOPE THIS book was a helpful resource for you and your students, or for those within your community or organization. I wish all Quetzal Mamas and Papas success in their endeavors, and I am counting on you to ensure our Latino students earn admission to the best colleges.

Tip! This book has been translated *en Español* and is available on Amazon and Barnes & Noble.

Join the Quetzal Mama Community – The Quetzal Mama community is a national group of parents, students, community-based organizations, and non-profits, who support the Quetzal Mama mission. This community is online via Facebook and Twitter. Google "Quetzal Mama" and you will find us. Join our community!

Bring Quetzal Mama to Your School or Organization – If you would like to bring Quetzal Mama to your local school district, high school, college-going program, or community based organization, contact quetzalmama@gmail.com. Quetzal Mama provides more than 75 workshop topics, 5-day boot camps for 5th grade to 12th grade students, professional development seminars for faculty and staff, as well as a workshop series designed exclusively for parents.

Support the Quetzal Mama Mission – Quetzal Mama provides *pro bono* programs and services, year-round, to low-income, first generation, Latino students. One hundred percent of book sales, speaking fees, and donations go directly to fund the pro bono programs. Why not contribute to our community so that more deserving students can receive exceptional college admission coaching? To find out how to donate to the Quetzal Mama mission, send an email to quetzalmama@gmail.com.

Tell Other Parents! If you enjoyed this book, I would appreciate a customer review on Amazon.com, Barnesandnoble.com, or Goodreads. com. If this book is not stocked in your school district, public library, or Migrant Education office, ask them to stock it! This will enable others in your community to receive valuable advice. Let's empower each other so that our Latino children can take flight and soar! ¡Sí se puede Quetzal Mamas!

—Roxanne Ocampo "Quetzal Mama"

REFERENCES

1. Ceballo, Rosario. *From Barrios to Yale: The Role of Parenting Strategies in Latino Families.* University of Michigan. *Hispanic Journal of Behavioral Sciences,* Vol. 26 No. 2, May 2004.

2. Cohen, Geoffrey L., and Garcia, Julio. *Identity, Belonging, and Achievement : A Model, Interventions, Implications.* Current Directions in Psychological Science 2008 17: 365-369, December 2008.

3. Cohen, Geoffrey L., et. al. *Recursive Processes in Self-Affirmation: Intervening to Close the Minority Achievement Gap.* Science, Vol. 324, No. 5925, pp. 400-403, April, 2009.

4. Quiñones-Hinojosa, Dr. Alfredo, email message to author, May 2, 2012.

5. Quiñones-Hinojosa, Dr. Alfredo, *Becoming Dr. Q: My Journey from Migrant Farm Worker to Brain Surgeon.* California: University of California Press, 2011.

6. Rodriguez, Gloria G., Ph.D. *Raising Nuestros Niños: Bringing Up Latino Children in a Bicultural World.* New York: Fireside, 1999.

7. Sedlacek, William E.: *Beyond the Big Test: Noncognitive Assessment in Higher Education.* San Francisco, CA: Jossey Bass, 2004.

8. "Self Affirmation." Oxford Dictionary. Available online:

9. http://oxforddictionaries.com/definition/self-affirmation?region =us&q=self+affirmation; Access date: May 3, 2016.

10. University of California Freshman Profile accessed at http://admission.universityofcalifornia.edu/freshman/profiles/

Glossary

80-10-10 Rule – Quetzal Mama's rule of thumb designed to help students maximize odds of admission. Students should apply to 80% "match" schools; 10% "reach" schools; and 10% "safety" schools.

AB540 – AB 540 is Assembly Bill 540, signed into law on October 12, 2001, by California Governor Gray Davis. It is adopted in California Education Code § 68130.5 and is a California state law that allows qualifying *undocumented* students to pay in-state tuition at state colleges.

ACT – The American College Testing (ACT) exam tests students in English, mathematics, reading, and science. There is also an optional 30-minute essay portion. Students may take this examination in lieu of the SAT. Colleges use the ACT as an assessment tool for admission consideration. See Chapter 14, "*College Entrance Exams.*"

Advanced Placement (or "AP") – High school classes designated as college preparatory and are weighted for GPA and class ranking purposes. AP examinations may be taken after completing respective coursework. See Chapter 12, "*Course Selection.*"

Affirmative Action – Positive, pro-active steps taken for admission purposes, by a college or university, that contribute toward equal access for historically underrepresented minorities who have been historically excluded or underrepresented in higher education.

AP and IB Examinations – Advanced Placement (AP) examinations and International Baccalaureate (IB) examinations are examinations that correspond to high school coursework. AP examinations are administered by the College Board each May, while IB examinations are administered through the International Baccalaureate Organization each May and November. See Chapter 12, "*Course Selection*," and Chapter 14, "*College Entrance Exams*."

Ave Enjaulada – In reference to Quetzal Mama's dicho: "*Ave que no vuela, es ave enjaulada*." This refers to Latino parents who insist their daughters attend college close to home. See Chapter 11, "*Ave Enjaulada*."

Bachelor's Degree – An undergraduate degree offered by 4-year colleges and universities. Depending on the major, some students will earn a Bachelor of Arts or a Bachelor of Science Degree.

Big Four – Quetzal Mama's four critical components simultaneously required for graduation, college preparation, discipline-specific preparation, and private/competitive university preparation. See Chapter 8, "*Set Up a Game Plan*."

Blind Letter – A Letter of Recommendation (LOC) written by an evaluator where the student is not allowed to know the contents (positive or negative). See Chapter 15, "*Letters of Recommendation*."

Class Rank – Class rank is a calculated measurement, based exclusively on your student's academic performance relative to other students in his/her class. The high school Registrar calculates class rank based on several factors including weighted courses (e.g., AP and IB courses), specific grade-levels (e.g., tenth- through twelfth-grade courses), and other factors specific to the academic institution. Most selective colleges and universities will carefully review student's GPA and class rank, with particular attention to the *weighted* GPA. Weighted rank factors the Honors and AP/IB courses (those that are considered the most difficult).

College Board – A non-profit organization that administers several programs for students including Advanced Placement (AP), the PSAT, SAT, and the SAT Subject tests.

Common Application – This is an online application utilized by nearly all private and competitive universities (including Ivy League schools). Students complete and submit to any of the participating 500+ member colleges and universities. Find them at www.commonapp.org.

Community College – Also known as "Junior College." A Community College is a two-year institution of higher education that offers transfer curriculum, Associate Degree programs, and/or coursework with credits transferable toward a bachelor's degree at a four-year college. Additionally, community colleges offer occupational or technical curriculum designed to prepare students for employment in two years.**CSS Profile** –This is an online application, administered by The College Board that collects financial information from students on behalf of approximately 400 colleges and scholarship programs. This profile is in addition to the FAFSA.

Cultural Authenticity – A student who has developed a cultural identity based on *authentic* life experiences within a cultural group and identifies positively with this group. See Chapter 13, "*Extracurricular Activities.*"

Cyber Profile – A student's public, online presence, known as a digital "footprint." The profile represents student's activity in various social media platforms such as Facebook, YouTube, Instagram, and Twitter to name a few. Many admissions teams will review a student's profile prior to making admission decisions. Therefore, parents should help their student "clean up" and remove questionable images or posts, in order to create a positive and marketable profile.

DACA (Deferred Action for Childhood Arrivals) – While DACA students are not eligible (at this time) for Federal Aid, they may be eligible for State aid. There is a growing list of universities offering "Tuition Equity" for undocumented students. For a complete and up-to-date list, visit unitedwedream.org.

Deferral – When a student is "deferred" it means the admission office has not yet received all candidate materials, and is therefore, deferring the decision until they can adequately assess the candidate. This is different from being "Waitlisted."

DREAM Act – Development, Relief, and Education for Alien Minors Act. This legislation was introduced to Congress in 2001, but has yet to pass. However, in California – Effective January 1, 2012, AB 130 allows California students who meet the in-state tuition requirements to apply for and receive scholarships derived from non-public funds. Effective January 1, 2013, AB 131, allows eligible AB540 students to receive some state scholarships. Other states may have laws similar to California's AB130 & AB131. For more information visit UnitedWeDream.org, e4fc. org, Maldef.org, or NCLR.org. To view scholarships for AB540 students, visit www.quetzalmama.com.

Early Action – This option allows students to submit college applications by November 1 at midnight to apply "Early." Early Action provides few restrictions and many advantages, including a statistical edge. This option is not to be confused with Early Decision. See Chapter 16, "*Early versus Regular Decision.*"

Early Decision – This option is different from Early Action in that it is a *binding* and has financial implications. See Chapter 16, "*Early Action versus Regular Decision.*"

EFC (Estimated Family Contribution) – The EFC is a calculation of a family's ability to contribute toward the student's college expenses. It is the number used by the college to calculate and determine the amount of federal aid the student is eligible to receive. The EFC is not the amount the family must pay for college or the amount of aid a student will receive.

Extracurricular Activities – These are non-classroom activities that can contribute to a well-rounded education. They can include such activities as athletics, clubs, student government, recreational and social organizations, and events. See Chapter 13, "*Extracurricular Activities.*"

FAFSA – Free Application for Federal Student Aid. See www.fafsa.gov.

Fee Waiver – The waiver, provided by the school guidance counselor, the college/university, or the College Board, eliminates payment of a fee. For example, a student may request a fee waiver for the PSAT or SAT exam. Or, the student may request a fee waiver for the college application.

Financial Aid –To gain a better understanding of the basics of financial aid, visit www.studentaid.ed.gov and also www.fafsa.ed.gov.

First Generation Student – Students whose parents did not complete/ graduate from a 4-year college. This definition includes students who may have older siblings who are current college students and/or graduates, but they still belong to the first generation within their respective family to attend college.

Fly-In Programs – A select group of universities will cover the round-trip costs and lodging for high school students who may be potential college recruits. The goal of these programs is to recruit more diverse candidates and are intended to familiarize the student with the campus, culture, and financial aid aspects. There are many selective colleges that host Fly-In Programs including MIT, Yale, and Johns Hopkins.

Freedom of Information Act (FOIA) – This federal law allows parents to request and to obtain certain documents from a pre-school, public or private elementary school, or secondary school. See Chapter 5, "*Work the System.*"

GATE – A state-funded program in public K-12 schools for intellectually "gifted" students. See Chapter 5, *"Work the System."*

Geographic Diversity – A strategy by applicants to cast a wider net of colleges being considered to those more than 500 miles away (or out of state). This is an admissions strategy because colleges are often seeking geographically diverse candidates to diversity their incoming freshman pool.

GPA (Grade Point Average) – A student's grade point average is found by adding the total grade point values for all courses completed in high school and dividing by the total number of credits. For example, an A = 4 points; B = 3 points; C = 2; D = 1; and F = 0. The GPA may be weighted or unweighted.

Grant – A monetary (financial) award given to a student to help pay college expenses. Grants are usually not repaid by the student.

Hispanic Serving Institution (HSI) – A college, university, or District where the total enrollment of students is at least 25% Hispanic. Designation of HSI status and funding is by the Federal Government, through grants to assist first generation, low income Hispanic students.

Historically Underrepresented or Minority Student – A student who belongs to a racial and ethnic population that is underrepresented in higher education, relative to their numbers in the general population. Specifically, we are referring to African Americans, Mexican-Americans, Native Americans (American Indians, Alaska Natives, and Native Hawaiians), Pacific Islanders, and mainland Puerto Ricans.

IB – International Baccalaureate (IB) is a challenging two-year high school program that may lead to an IB Diploma. See Chapter 14, *"College Entrance Exams."*

Ignacia la Ingeniosa – This term describes a resourceful personality type that reads books, researches websites, talks with teachers and parents, in order to help secure resources for her children. See Chapter 7, *"Ignacia la Ingeniosa."*

Impacted – This refers to academic majors or programs considered highly selective at a college or university because the number of applicants is significantly higher than the number of students admitted in a given year.

Ivy League – The Ivy League started as an athletic conference in 1954 that included eight private colleges including Brown University, Columbia University, Cornell University, Dartmouth College, Harvard University, Princeton University, the University of Pennsylvania, and Yale University. Today the Ivy League represents the most prestigious, selective, and competitive colleges to gain admission.

Legacy Applicant – A college applicant who receives admission preference by a college or university on the basis of their historical family relationship (usually a parent or grandparent) to the institution.

Letter of Recommendation – A letter required by many, but not all, colleges and universities. The letter is one of many components of the college application. See Chapter 15, *"Letters of Recommendation."*

Liberal Arts College – A degree-granting institution where the academic focus is on developing the intellect and broad instruction in the humanities and sciences, versus professional, vocational, or technical training.

Likely Letter – An extremely rare letter from highly selective private universities, sent to the very strongest candidates in their applicant pool. The letter is sent far in advance of the regular decision notification process, and will say that although the university is barred from providing such an early official acceptance letter (due to legal regulations), it is an unofficial admission decision.

Major/Minor – A major is a student's field of study (or discipline) in college, often leading to a particular degree. Examples of common college majors include engineering, pre-med, political science, etc. A minor is a secondary field of study (or discipline) in college.

National Hispanic Scholar – The National Hispanic Recognition Program (NHRP) administered by the College Board identifies high-performing U.S. Hispanic students based on a combination of their PSAT score and grade point average. Students earning this distinction may receive financial incentives from various colleges and universities. See Chapter 14, "*College Entrance Exams*."

Need-Blind Admission – A college admissions policy whereby colleges make admission decisions without considering the financial circumstances of applicants.

Online Classes – Online classes meet through an online connection where students participate through an online learning management system. Students access and participate in course lectures, correspond with classmates and instructors, and submit coursework through the online connection.

Overmatching – Refers to mid-level performing, college-ready students who apply for admission to colleges or universities where they are under-qualified (their academic profile is below the profile of admitted students).

Personal Statement – The term identifies a required essay included in the student's application to a college or university. See Chapter 17, "*The Personal Statement*."

Prerequisite Courses –This is a condition or requirement that must be met before enrolling in a course. To satisfy a prerequisite, students must typically receive a "C" or better in the course to advance to the next class.

Priority Dates – A date established by the FAFSA when students must have their FAFSA completed and filed in order to be considered for financial aid. Typically, the priority date is March 2. However, check this site to confirm your state's deadline: https://fafsa.ed.gov/deadlines.htm#

Private College or University – Private colleges and universities rely on income from an endowment, private donations, religious or other organizations, and student tuition.

Prompt – A prompt is a question or statement, generally contained in a college application or scholarship application, and requires the student to respond in written (essay) form.

PSAT – Preliminary SAT/National Merit Scholarship Qualifying Test is an exam taken in the tenth and eleventh grades and commonly referred to as PSAT. It helps students prepare for the SAT and measures three areas: critical reading skills, math problem-solving skills and writing skills. See also Chapter 14 "*College Entrance Exams.*"

Public College or University – Public institutions primarily receive funding from the state or other governmental entities and are administered by public boards.

QuestBridge – A national non-profit program that connects high-achieving, low-income students with "full-ride" college scholarships and educational opportunities through partnerships with leading U.S. colleges and universities.

Quetzal Mama – The term identifies a proud Latina mom who will do anything to ensure her children fulfill their chosen path. She provides her children with every opportunity for success and removes all barriers. A Quetzal Mama knows her children have unique gifts and talents and will make a profound contribution to society. See Chapter 1, *"What Is a Quetzal Mama?"* Quetzal Mama is also the pen name of the author, Roxanne Ocampo.

Quetzal Mama Principles – These 10 principles represent a philosophical approach to nurturing and raising our future Latino leaders. See Chapter 3, *"The 10 Quetzal Mama Principles."*

Rank (Class Rank) –A numeric measurement of where your student performs academically, relative to other students in his/her class, based on GPA.

Reach School – Defined as a campus where the student's academic profile is moderately below the average profile of admitted students. See Chapter 18, *"How to Select the Right College."*

Rolling Admission –An admission practice used by some colleges to review and complete applications as they arrive, rather than according to a set deadline. Students generally receive admissions decisions quickly from colleges with a rolling admission process.

Safety School – This is a college where a student will likely be admitted because the student's academic profile is superior to the profile of admitted students. See Chapter 18, *"How to Select the Right College."*

SAR – The Student Aid Report (SAR) outlines your financial status and is what universities use to document your student aid.

SAT – Scholastic Aptitude Test is an exam administered by the College Board, testing critical reading, writing, and math. See Chapter 14, *"College Entrance Exams."*

SAT Subject Test – A one-hour, multiple choice examination administered by the College Board that measures a student's knowledge in one of 20 subject areas. See Chapter 14, "*College Entrance Exams.*"

Selective College or University – A campus where the odds of admission are very low, and are based on factors such as ACT or SAT scores, GPA and class rank, amongst other factors.

SIR – The "Statement of Intent to Register," is the official declaration by the student confirming formal acceptance of the admission offer and intent to attend the particular college. The SIR due date is May 1.

Student Aid Report (SAR) – A Student Aid Report (SAR) is a document that contains the student's Expected Family Contribution (EFC). Colleges use this contribution number to determine eligibility for financial aid based on the school's cost of attendance.

Transcript – A cumulative record of a student's academic history that includes courses completed, weighted and un-weighted GPA, Honors designation, recognition programs, state proficiency exam scores (if applicable in your state), ACT and/or SAT and Subject Matter test scores, and AP and IB test scores.

Undermatching – Refers to high-performing, college ready students who select and enroll in colleges with selectivity levels significantly lower than their academic profile or forego applying to college altogether.

Universal College Application – This is a standard application accepted by 45+ colleges that are Universal College Application members, found at: www.universalcollegeapp.com.

Un-Weighted GPA – This is the calculated average of the student's cumulative high school grades based on a standard 4.0 scale. Most colleges will review your weighted and un-weighted GPA.

Valedictorian – The title is conferred upon the highest academically ranked student within a graduating high school class. This student traditionally delivers the keynote speech at the graduation commencement.

Waitlist – A list of college applicants who are not admitted nor denied, but instead, "waitlisted." This happens when selective colleges cannot accurately predict their yield, and therefore retain a small roster of students who may be admitted after a particular date. This is not the same as being "Deferred."

Weighted GPA – These are extra points or "weight" added to a standard GPA. The weighting factors and calculates classes that are considered more challenging such as AP, IB, or Honors courses.

Work-Study Program – An on-campus, part time job, offered by some colleges during the school year as part of their financial aid package. Monies earned from work study are typically used to pay for tuition or other college charges.

Yield – The percentage of students who accept a respective college's offer of admission and enroll or "matriculate" in that college.

Made in the USA
San Bernardino, CA
08 August 2016